It is easy in this day and a~~g~~
and to allow those misconc
relationship with Him. R....... ....uny weaves together
depth of insight into the text, well-articulated illustrations, and
thought provoking questions. The reader will come away with
a renewed understanding of God that will drive a deeper love
for Him than they thought possible. Whether you are a learned
scholar or just exploring the faith, this book will transform
your understanding of and adoration to God. My family,
including three teenagers, have begun using this book as part
of our weekly family devotions.

Dana Allin
Synod Executive, ECO-Presbyterians

I love that Richard Gibbons writes this book with such a clear
expectation that I will see and meet and be transformed anew
by Almighty God through the spiritual treasures of Psalm 139.
I love that he writes with a theological depth that trembles. I love
that he reaches from the psalm out across the Scriptures to help
us see the astonishing breadth of God's saving, transforming
purposes. I love how practical and readable this book is –
I hear the voice of a pastor in every page, spurring us on with
truths that will lodge God-wrought hope and holiness into the
reality of our fraught, fragile lives. If you love the Psalms – and
especially Psalm 139 – then read *Conspiracy Theory!*

Colin Buchanan
Christian Children's Recording artist and author, Sydney,
Australia

As a pastor for more than three decades I have met, counselled,
and prayed for countless individuals who feel God is, in some
way, against them. 'Somebody up there must hate me,' is the

half humorous, half tragic response made when life takes a hard, confusing, or tragic turn. Richard Gibbons addresses this fear directly with warmth, wisdom, and compassion. Using the most beautiful Psalm 139 Richard unveils that 'the someone up there' is the tender and loving God who not only created us but constantly watches over us. This book winsomely reveals that God is not against us but for us and ever working to shape us into his beloved children. I sincerely wish I had had this book to give to the countless number of people who came needing to hear its message of God's loving presence and constant care.

Mark R. Patterson
Director, Flourish Institute: School of Ministry

This is a warm, practical, encouraging Bible-soaked book for any believer about what used to be regarded as elements of a 'normal' Christian life – in other words, one with perplexity, challenge, heartache and darkness, but nonetheless a trust that God is somehow at work even when we don't understand what is happening to us. I'm pleased to commend it.

David Baker
Editor, *Evangelicals Now*

Richard Gibbons emerges as one of our nation's strongest Bible teachers, leading a thriving ministry in the heart of Greenville, South Carolina. While we can't all sit under his preaching, we can be enriched by his devotional journey into Psalm 139. Shall the Word of God be plumbed to its depths? Never. But warm devotion and faithful doctrine take us deeper and deeper into each verse of this transformational Psalm, growing our confidence that God is good even when life is hard.

Tim McConnell
Pastor, First Presbyterian Church, Colorado Springs, Colorado
Author of *Happy Church: Pursuing Radical Joy as the People of God*

Wit is hugely underrated when it comes to writing and teaching/preaching. However, sharing a good story, even a funny one, is not the end in itself, it is a means of drawing readers and listeners in. Richard has always possessed a sharp wit and ability to tell a good story well and this comes across again and again throughout this book, but never once takes us away from Psalm 139.

This is a book that is suitable for both the believer and the genuine spiritual seeker. If you want to grow deeper in your relationship with God, read this book! If you're genuinely seeking and want to find out more about God, read this book! The questions at the end of each chapter are very helpful for both believer and spiritual seeker alike. Whether you're a follower or seeker of God, Richard closes by reminding us of the question that Jesus asks of every person: 'Do you love me?'

Alistair Purss
Lead Pastor, Dumfries Baptist Church, Scotland

Facing external challenges or internal struggles, Christians can sometimes become bewildered by God's actions and even doubtful of His care. With warm and wise reflections on one of the greatest songs ever written, coupled with engaging examples from across scripture, Dr Gibbons applies key truths about God's character and purposes in ways which are profound yet personal, and challenging yet life-changing, showing us how much God knows, cares, acts and loves.

Jonathan Lamb
Writer, teacher and minister-at-large, Keswick Ministries

CONSPIRACY THEORY

When God is
Seemingly
Against Us

RICHARD GIBBONS

CHRISTIAN
FOCUS

Copyright © Richard Gibbons 2021

Paperback ISBN 978-1-5271-0726-7
Ebook ISBN 978-1-5271-0853-0

10 9 8 7 6 5 4 3 2 1

Published in 2021
by
Christian Focus Publications Ltd,
Geanies House, Fearn, Ross-shire,
IV20 1TW, United Kingdom.

www.christianfocus.com

Cover design by James Amour

Printed and bound by
Bell & Bain, Glasgow

CONTENTS

ACKNOWLEDGEMENTS

Over the last few years as I have been immersed in writing *Conspiracy Theory*, my lovely wife Ruth has consistently encouraged me while displaying incredible patience and focused prayer. Ruth and our son Michael have sacrificed a great deal over the years to allow me to be involved in ministry, and I am eternally grateful for their unceasing and exceptional love and support.

My congregation and the staff at First Presbyterian Church in Greenville, in South Carolina, are remarkably dedicated and committed. They are not only longsuffering each Sunday, but are exceedingly gracious and supportive, as they faithfully continue to serve Him 'who first loved us.'

Finally, I owe a debt of gratitude I will never be able to pay to my assistant Lynn Johnson, along with Tomi Wier and

Marcie Lemley of the church's communications department. I have stretched their patience to breaking point on multiple occasions as I have written and then rewritten each chapter. Jim Holmes, of Great Writing, has also displayed infinite patience as a first-rate editor, as has David Dykes whose expertise and experience as a professional writer and advisor has proven to be invaluable. I am grateful to God for each of them.

PREFACE

(Read this it is important)

If you have ever struggled with deep disappointments, unanswered prayers, or found your life crumbling around you, and feeling as if God is conspiring against you, *Conspiracy Theory* was written just for you.

For many of us life is dominated by a mild addiction to an image-rich, digital playground where meaning and purpose are determined by how connected we are to the ubiquitous convenience of a digital lifestyle. The immense popularity of current social network sites like Twitter, Instagram, TikTok, and Facebook reveal that connectedness and intimacy are priorities for all of us. Yet, for all of the technological sophistication available, there is also a deep-seated awareness that there is so much more to life than a digital existence.

Conspiracy Theory seeks to draw you into a fresh understanding of the outrageous love and extravagant grace encountered in the life-transforming nature of God. It quickly takes you to a level which enlarges the mind and warms the heart as you begin to immerse yourself in one of the best loved psalms of all time, Psalm 139. In doing so you will discover that you find yourself engaging with God as He truly is; such an experience is not for the faint-hearted.

To instinctively focus on God before focusing on yourself will challenge you and cause you to radically reconsider how you live and what it is that defines you. More importantly, you will learn that moving to a new level of intimacy in your relationship with God is personally engaging and deeply transformative, leaving you with a passionate, constructive preoccupation with God Himself. This level of intimacy will help shape and fashion your appreciation of who God really is, and cause you to wrestle with the greatest single need in the life of any individual: to grasp and then grapple with a mature, understanding of the majesty, grace, grandeur, and radiance of the overwhelming love of God.

But please be careful, you may find that as God conspires to draw you into a deeper engagement you radically reframe or reinterpret the quality of your relationship with Him. You may also discover that you are prayerfully asking some fearless, searching, spiritual questions at an entirely new level. Answering the questions at the end of each chapter will allow you to explore the life-changing principles contained in Psalm 139. They will, however, challenge you deeply and personally.

Psalm 139

For the director of music. Of David. A psalm.

¹ O Lᴏʀᴅ, you have searched me and you know me.
² You know when I sit and when I rise;
  you perceive my thoughts from afar.
³ You discern my going out and my lying down;
  you are familiar with all my ways.
⁴ Before a word is on my tongue
  you know it completely, O Lᴏʀᴅ.
⁵ You hem me in — behind and before;
  you have laid your hand upon me.
⁶ Such knowledge is too wonderful for me,
  too lofty for me to attain.
⁷ Where can I go from your Spirit?
  Where can I flee from your presence?
⁸ If I go up to the heavens, you are there;
if I make my bed in the depths, you are there.
⁹ If I rise on the wings of the dawn,
  if I settle on the far side of the sea,
¹⁰ even there your hand will guide me,
  your right hand will hold me fast.
¹¹ If I say, 'Surely the darkness will hide me
  and the light become night around me,'
¹² even the darkness will not be dark to you;
  the night will shine like the day,
  for darkness is as light to you.
¹³ For you created my inmost being;
you knit me together in my mother's womb.
¹⁴ I praise you because I am fearfully and wonderfully made;
your works are wonderful, I know that full well.
¹⁵ My frame was not hidden from you
  when I was made in the secret place.
When I was woven together in the depths of the earth,

¹⁶ your eyes saw my unformed body.
All the days ordained for me
were written in your book
before one of them came to be.
¹⁷ How precious to me are your thoughts, O God!
How vast is the sum of them!
¹⁸ Were I to count them,
they would outnumber the grains of sand.
When I awake, I am still with you.
¹⁹ If only you would slay the wicked, O God!
Away from me, you bloodthirsty men!
²⁰ They speak of you with evil intent;
your adversaries misuse your name.
²¹ Do I not hate those who hate you, O Lord,
and abhor those who rise up against you?
²² I have nothing but hatred for them;
I count them my enemies.
²³ Search me, O God, and know my heart;
test me and know my anxious thoughts.
²⁴ See if there is any offensive way in me,
and lead me in the way everlasting.

1

SURPRISED AND ASTONISHED

For the director of music. Of David.

*O LORD, you have searched me and you know me
You know when I sit and when I rise;
you perceive my thoughts from afar.*
(Ps. 139:1–2)

Surprise

Some years ago I met a friend and asked about his family. He replied that earlier that day his wife Catherine had gone into a busy coffee shop, ordered a latte and a Kit Kat, and sat down at one of the last remaining tables. A few minutes later, another customer, unable to find a seat elsewhere, sat down beside her. He looked over, exchanged a smile, but said nothing. After a moment or two he paused from reading his newspaper and, much to Catherine's surprise, picked up the Kit Kat, broke off a piece, and began to eat it. Catherine was seriously uncertain as to what was going on but was determined not to be taken advantage of. With considerable determination, she picked up the Kit Kat, broke off another piece, and began to eat. Looking somewhat surprised, the man took the third piece; undeterred, Catherine ate the final piece and still nothing was said.

After a few moments the man got up, walked over to the counter, purchased a pastry, and sat at an empty table as far from Catherine as he could. Two or three minutes later, Catherine, now feeling a little uncomfortable, finished her coffee and decided she should leave. As she rose to leave, however, something in her changed. She looked over at the man's table, realized he had quartered his pastry, and knowing she would have to pass that table on the way out, Catherine came to a decision. As she made her way to the door, she reached out, lifted a piece of the pastry and popped it into her mouth. She then smiled, nodded to the man, and left the coffee shop.

As she walked away, feeling strangely satisfied by her action and realizing her fingers were a little sticky from the pastry, she put her hand in her pocket for a tissue. To her complete surprise and deep embarrassment, she discovered her own Kit Kat.

Now pause for a moment and consider what was going on in Catherine's mind when she put her hand in her pocket. In that fleeting second when her hand touched her own Kit Kat, I imagine she found it difficult to process exactly what was going on. Her mind would find it difficult to deal with what had just occurred. Yet, paradoxically, her dilemma was clear. Suddenly, what she thought had happened turned out to be very different from what in fact had happened.

Now consider what was going through the man's mind. How was he processing what had just occurred? He had gone into a coffee shop to relax for a few minutes, and a strange woman, without asking permission, took a piece of his Kit Kat—not once, but twice. When he had made it very plain that he wished to have nothing more to do with her, she accosted him a second time by stealing a piece of his pastry.

My reason for beginning with this story is to ask you a question: When was the last time you were truly surprised? Not a gentle, 'I did not see that coming' type of surprise, but a jaw-dropping, overwhelming, *Wow!* type of surprise. From time to time you may have been surprised at Christmas or on your birthday or perhaps a situation you were concerned about turned out to be much better than you initially imagined. But how would you respond if God was the One behind the wow! type of surprise?

There are other occasions when we face complex and difficult circumstances that are out of our control. Circumstances no one could have seen coming. In early 2020, countries around the world experienced a global pandemic that resulted in a significant loss of life, extraordinary challenges to health care systems, the closing of businesses, schools and colleges, postponed weddings, cancelled graduations, substantial unemployment, and ailing economies. How then should you respond when things do not go the way you had planned, and it seems as if God is conspiring against you?

My hope for you as you read through this book and explore the hidden depths of Psalm 139 is that God will surprise you in such a way that He will draw you into a deeper relationship with Himself and that you will come to a fresh understanding and deeper appreciation of Him. But don't be surprised if He takes you to places you had not previously imagined and challenges you in the circumstances you are facing while equipping and enabling you to respond to what you once thought was impossible.

Understanding the Challenge

As you begin to read this book, your first surprise may be that you are actually reading it. Perhaps a friend has given it to you as a gift; possibly you are reading it as part of a Bible study group; or it may be that you simply have a desire to grow in your faith. Regardless of your motive, you may be surprised to be reading a book that focuses on a psalm from the Old Testament.

Some years ago Philip Yancey wrote an excellent book, *The Bible Jesus Read*. In it he recalls how surprised he was when reading some of Shakespeare's plays. As he described his experience of having to adjust to the archaic language of Elizabethan English and the awkwardness of reading a play, Yancey's readers would have immediately returned to their own teenage years of being in school when they were given *Macbeth* or *Julius Caesar* for a class assignment. Like Yancey, readers of Shakespeare would have found it difficult to adjust to the new experience of immersing themselves in eleventh-century Scotland or ancient Rome as initially it seemed to have little to teach them about life today. What readers of Shakespeare's plays discover, however, is his writing is not simply about a historical context filled with unpronounceable names and unfamiliar places, but a world infected with the tranquilizing addiction of greed, ambition, paranoia, and an uncontrollable lust for power. The surprising thing for many readers of Shakespeare is that, in reading his plays, you learn a great deal about yourself.

As you begin to explore Psalm 139, you will also discover that although you live in a world dominated by the ubiquitous digital convenience of smartphones, iPads, Facebook, and YouTube, the intimacy contained within this psalm has a great deal to teach us about living the Christian life in a twenty-first century environment, where the temporary and the transient nature of a virtual existence promises so much, yet often leaves us with so little.

If you are serious about growing in your faith and are ready to prayerfully ask some fearless, searching questions about your relationship with God, come and explore with me the depths of teaching in Psalm 139. In the process you may well discover the refining and shaping hand of God at work in your life. You may begin to think of Him in an entirely new way. You may come to realize that in the deepest recesses of your life things are changing. Moments of personal intimacy with Him will be more frequent and intense. Prayer will become much more meaningful. Passages from this psalm will bring a new significance to your life as you discover a greater understanding of Him and a longing to be more Christlike in your daily living. This journey may turn out to be quite a surprise.

The Significance of the Psalms

The Book of Psalms contains some of the most memorized passages in the entire Bible. Jesus was so familiar with the psalms that they occupied a large place in His life and teaching. It was the prayer-book which He would use in the synagogue service, and His hymn-book in the Temple festival. He used it in His teaching, met temptation with it, sang the Hallel from it after the Last Supper, quoted it from the cross, and died with it on His lips.[1]

As you begin to read the psalms, you will discover fairly quickly that there are different classifications within them. Of the 150, there are Psalms of Ascent and Psalms of Lament, Messianic Psalms (which highlight aspects of the life, death, and ministry of Christ), psalms of praise and thanksgiving, Royal Psalms of affirmation and trust, Wisdom Psalms, and Penitential Psalms.

1. J. G. S. S. Thomson and F. D. Kidner, *Psalms, the New Bible Dictionary* 3rd Edition (Leicester, England: Inter Varsity Press, 1996), (Libronix Digital Library CD-Rom).

Yet it is neither the technical side of their classifications, nor the literary devices that the Hebrew language employs that draws us to the psalms. We are drawn to them because we find within them prayers we can identify with, circumstances we understand, and trials and difficulties we recognize. In the midst of all of this, however, the psalms provide for us words of hope, comfort, and transformation. Derek Kidner, in recognizing the value of the psalms, writes:

> Here are mirrored the ideals of religious piety and communion with God, of sorrow for sin and the search for perfection, of walking in darkness, unafraid, by the lamp of faith; of obedience to the law of God, delight in the worship of God, fellowship with the friends of God, reverence for the Word of God; of humility under the chastening rod, trust when evil triumphs and wickedness prospers, serenity in the midst of storm.[2]

Psalm 139 has a great deal to teach us about living life to the fullest today.

First Things First: 'O Lord'

Several years ago Starbucks became incredibly popular. Coffee drinkers across the nation discovered that if they were to explore the 'Starbucks experience' it felt as if they would need to learn a new vocabulary to order a cup of coffee. Now, however, we easily order 'a latte-grande, no foam, skinny milk, extra hot with a solo shot,' and think nothing of it. In the midst of such daily challenges, most of us discover that if we are open enough to explore new possibilities they just might introduce us to experiences we never thought possible. In exploring Psalm 139 there may be moments when you feel out of your comfort

---

2. Ibid.

zone as you wrestle with new concepts and unfamiliar terms, but please persevere; being open to new experiences is often a healthy experience.

The title of this psalm tells us that it was written by David, who was arguably Israel's greatest king and is famously known as being 'a man after God's own heart' (Acts 13:22). During his lifetime David wrote many of the best-known psalms—approximately 73 of the 150 psalms are attributed to him.

Here in Psalm 139, he begins in a surprising way: instead of concentrating on the circumstances of his own life or the challenges he was facing, his focus is elsewhere. The opening words tell us that David's heart was concentrating on the LORD. It is these first two words, 'O LORD,' that set the tone, focus, purpose, and direction for the rest of the psalm, and we see this repeated in verses 4 and 21. By focusing on his relationship with the Lord, David sets the same tone when beginning what is often considered the most intimate of all the psalms: 'The LORD is my Shepherd' (Ps. 23:1).

David's opening words encourage his readers to courageously engage with God as He truly is. If you are seeking to do the same, please remember this—that such an experience is not for the faint-hearted. To focus on Him before we focus on ourselves can challenge us very deeply and cause us to radically reconsider how we think of God.

When we pray, the temptation often is to focus on our own needs, the circumstances of our lives, the challenges we face, and the issues important to us. David, however, does the opposite. Reflected within his opening words, 'O LORD,' David sets a priority in prayer that is of fundamental importance if we are ever to grow in our faith. He insists that we focus on God first, by reminding his readers that whenever we engage with God, a deep and reverent sense of worship must lie at the very center of that prayer.

Now pause for a second and ask yourself what comes to your mind when you hear the word 'worship.' Perhaps you think of a church service where the congregation seems to engage in little more than an external ritual, reflective of religious tradition, observance, and duty. Such an image usually comes across as dull, insipid, and uninspiring. Why, then, does David begin with worship? Perhaps he knows what many do not. Heartfelt genuine worship involves so much more than the popular caricature of what the word 'worship' suggests. Worship for David is always impactful and profoundly moving, taking us away from passivity, apathy, and indifference to a new and fresh appreciation of the greatness and majesty of God. William Temple (Archbishop of Canterbury from 1942 to 1944) accurately defined authentic, heart-warming, meaningful worship as:

> the submission of all of our nature to God, it is the quickening of our conscience by His holiness, the nourishment of our minds by His truth, the purifying of our imagination by His beauty, the opening of our hearts to His love and the submission of our will to His purpose. And all of this gathered up in adoration which is the greatest human expression of which we are capable. [3]

Genuine worship will always involve the submission of our nature, the quickening of our conscience, the nourishment of our mind, the purifying of our imagination, the opening of our heart, and the submission of our will, climaxing in adoration that is the 'greatest human expression of which we are capable.' Worship that is engaging and deeply transformative will leave us with a passionate, constructive preoccupation with God

---

3. *Nature, Man and God*, by William Temple, the Gifford Lectures delivered at the University of Glasgow in the academic years 1932-1933 and 1933-1934.

Himself. This kind of intimate experience shapes and fashions our appreciation of who God really is. It causes us to wrestle with the greatest single need in the life of any Christian: to grasp and grapple with a mature, biblical understanding of the majesty, grace, grandeur, greatness, eminence, splendor, and radiance of the love of our incomparable God. Such an experience is often seen in the lives of biblical characters who, much to their own surprise, came into profound contact with God in a way they could never have anticipated.

In the opening chapters of Luke's Gospel, which are known as the infancy narratives, Mary's response to the greetings of her cousin Elizabeth is one of adoration and worship. Both were clearly recipients of the surprising, all-encompassing grace of God, which moves Mary to respond in astonished praise, 'My soul glorifies the Lord and my spirit rejoices in God my Savior' (Luke 1:46). Mary's expression of worship is the natural, instinctive response of a heart touched by the life-transforming, love of God, which has come to be known as *The Magnificat* (Luke 1:46–55). Luke goes on to record similar experiences: Zechariah, *The Benedictus* (Luke 1:68–79); the angels, *Glory in Excelsis* (Luke 2:14); and the response of the elderly Simeon, when to his utter amazement, he recognized the significance of what it means to be holding the fulfillment of God's unfolding redemption in his arms, *The Nunc dimittis* (Luke 2:29-32). These brief examples remind us that when we find our lives transformed by the living God, the heartfelt worship we engage in moves us to a place where we are lost in the immensity of His love, refreshed and renewed in the concentrated brilliance of His glory, overwhelmed by His mercy, and moved to praise and adoration. All of this is wrapped up in David's experience of God and is reflected in his opening phrase when he begins with the words, 'O LORD' (Ps. 139:1).

When God Makes the First Move

If you have found yourself checking in for a flight recently, you will know that each passenger is required to go through security before boarding the aircraft. This often involves emptying your pockets, removing jackets, shoes, belts, watches and any laptops from your carry-on luggage. Having surrendered all your worldly goods to the potential vagaries of the conveyor belt, you step forward, hold your hands above your head, and are electronically screened. If you fail the inspection, you are asked to stand to one side while a security officer passes a 'wand' over the offending area. Most of us don't mind airport security, and we are comforted in the knowledge that each passenger has been thoroughly searched. The only irritating part of the process is the length of time it takes. What you are sure of, however, is this: you have been thoroughly searched and nothing is hidden from the close scrutiny of the TSA personnel.

When David continues verse one and writes, 'You have searched me and you know me,' he is describing an all-encompassing, intimate search infinitely greater than the comprehensive searching process conducted at airport security. David is not simply describing an external experience but an exhaustive search of the heart, mind, and soul. Here he recognizes that God searches him in a manner so profound that nothing in his life is hidden. There are no locked doors, no hidden rooms; no place is off limits to God.

When David writes, 'O LORD, you have searched me,' he reminds us that God has searched us intimately and thoroughly. Yet, unless we pay careful attention to these words, we may be in danger of missing a deeply significant theological truth that lies behind them. David is reminding his readers that it is God who is doing the searching—God is the One who takes the initiative. He is not sitting back disengaged and distant from us; David is telling us that the opposite is the case. God is the One

24

who is proactive in reaching out to us, and He does so much more often than we think of reaching out to Him. In doing so, God is consistently seeking to move us to a deeper, richer, and fuller understanding of who He is and of our relationship with Him.

The truth that God is the One who takes the initiative in drawing us to Himself is seen throughout the pages of Scripture. This truth is highlighted for us in considerable detail in the apostle Paul's letter to the church in Ephesus (Eph. 1:3–6). The remarkable truth clearly expressed by Paul in Ephesians and elsewhere (2 Thess. 2:13–14; 2 Tim. 1:9–10) is that 'before the creation of the world' God set His love and affection on His children and He is the One who actively engages us. He is the One who lovingly reaches out to us in such a way as to draw us into a relationship with Himself. He then nourishes that relationship through the pages of His Word in order that we might be more Christlike in our daily living. This process is often described by theologians as the eternal decrees of God, and is seen within the unfolding plan of His redemptive purposes and providential care (1 Thess. 1: 3–6; 1 Cor. 1:8–9; Phil. 1:6; 1 Thess. 5:23–24; 2 Tim. 1:12; 4:18).

The deep insight involved in this divine initiative is also demonstrated in the opening words of the Bible where we read of God's taking the initiative in creation: 'In the beginning God created' (Gen. 1:1). We are also reminded of God's taking the initiative in reaching out to an entire race of people:

> 'For I know the plans I have for you,' declares the LORD, 'plans to prosper you and not to harm you, plans to give you hope and a future. Then you will call upon me and come and pray to me, and I will listen to you. You will seek me and find me when you seek me with all your heart. I will be found by you,' declares the LORD (Jer. 29:11–14).

On a more personal basis, the apostle Paul, looking back at his own conversion experience, reflects that it was a divine initiative that sought him out: 'God, who set me apart from birth and called me by his grace...' (Gal. 1:15). God began to fulfill His own plans for Paul when He set him apart from birth. Yet incredible as it seems, each of these events pales into insignificance when we consider the best-known passage in all of Scripture, John 3:16. Once again we are reminded that it is God's initiative that lies behind the fullest demonstration of His love:

> For God so loved the world that he gave his one and only Son, that whoever believes in him shall not perish but have eternal life. For God did not send his Son into the world to condemn the world, but to save the world through him (John 3:16–17).

The truth reflected in David's words, 'You have searched me,' moves us to a new appreciation of God's loving initiative in our own lives and leaves us feeling as if we are examining a priceless antique and in the process we slowly begin to realize its true value when we pause long enough to consider in detail that it has a value way beyond what we first imagined.

You Know Me!

When David continues to draw his readers further into the opening words of Psalm 139 and writes, 'You know me,' he is not, as we have already seen, writing about a relationship that is based on a passing acquaintance. He is clearly teaching that God knows each of us comprehensively and nothing is hidden from Him as His knowledge of us is exhaustive in every sense.

One of the overwhelming and consistent truths of this psalm is that David longs for his readers to know God and appreciate the majesty, greatness, and grandeur of God Himself.

Each word and phrase have been carefully chosen by David to point us toward the transcendent nature of God which tells us that He reigns over and above His creation. Yet nonetheless He has an intimate knowledge of us, a knowledge that is exhaustive, infinite, eternal, and unchangeable. One of the most challenging, yet comforting, truths of the entire Bible is to realize that God is familiar with every thought that has gone through our minds from the moment of our conception. He is familiar with every hope and dream, every wish and passionate longing, every heartfelt desire and every motivation, that has encouraged us to action.

Since He knows us so well, He is not only aware of every passionate longing but also of each disappointment and painful memory: the moment in school when we were not selected for the football or baseball team; the social rejection of the cool kids in class; the person at college whom we really liked but who never noticed we existed; and the job interview that did not work out well and our speculative 'what ifs' that followed. He understands the pain of a broken engagement and the loss of a future so carefully planned. He knows the agony and tearful regrets of a failed marriage or the mind-numbing grief of losing a child.

Yet within David's words, 'You know me,' there is another side to the character of God. When David reminds his readers not only that God is present during the difficult times but also that He uses those times to refine and fashion us into the people He intends for us to become, one of the most reassuring lessons in the Christian life is that God is present not only in the tough times but also present in moments of great blessing and excitement. There may have been moments when He enabled and sustained you while you persevered against all odds and worked through the challenges that threatened to overwhelm you at college or at work. For some, there is the moment when you first fell in love and subsequently married the love of your life. He delights in bringing together a husband and wife who experience moments of tender intimacy; such an experience is nothing less than a gift from God Himself. Other such moments are experienced in the birth of a child that, humanly speaking, did not seem possible. Perhaps for you, it was the healing and wholeness He brought to the deep emotional wounds of the past. Maybe you have experienced the inexpressible freedom He brings from an addictive lifestyle that blighted and debilitated each area of your life it touched.

For the Christian, such knowledge, depth of understanding, and appreciation of God are birthed and sustained through the intimacy with Him found in the pages of His Word. These are precious, unforgettable moments when the truth of Scripture comes alive and brings with it the transforming knowledge that He loves you with an everlasting love. Such moments impact our lives profoundly and instill within us the reassuring truth that He will never abandon us to the circumstances of this life or the spiritual poverty of life without Him. There is a great deal contained in this most memorable of phrases, 'And you know me.'

He Knows it All

A well-known passage in the closing chapter of Luke's Gospel (24:13–35) recounts the afternoon of Easter Sunday when two heartbroken disciples who had not heard the news about the resurrection were walking to the village of Emmaus. As the narrative unfolds, a fascinating dialogue takes place between Jesus and these disciples who were kept from recognizing Him. He engages them in conversation, and they have the opportunity to paradoxically ask, 'Are you only a visitor to Jerusalem and do not know the things that have happened there in these days?' (24:18).

Throughout the conversation, interaction, challenge, dialogue, invitation, and friendship take place. Yet, the reader is also aware that the enabling of genuine inquiry and the encouragement of honest heartfelt questions are not enough to satisfy the questions the disciples are wrestling with. As Jesus interacts with the two disciples, He also explains in considerable detail 'what was said in all the Scriptures concerning himself' (Luke 24:26–27). As the passage develops, it becomes clear that Jesus was not content to leave His disciples as agnostics: explanation, revelation, and transformation also take place. It is a remarkable thing to consider that of all the places Jesus could have been on that first Easter Sunday afternoon, He wanted to be with disciples who were hurting, confused, and uncertain of all that had happened over the last few days.

This incident comes to a climax when the disciples' 'eyes were opened and they recognized him' (Luke 24:31). Recognizing who Jesus is and responding with transformed hearts, the disciples finally understand God's loving purposes and plans for humanity, and all that had lain at the very center of the crucifixion and resurrection. It is not surprising therefore when they say, 'Were not our hearts burning within us while he talked with us on the road and opened the Scriptures to us?' (Luke 24:32).

Jesus knew His disciples intimately. He understood and perceived their 'thoughts from afar.' He knew on that first Easter Sunday that the only way to deal with the dreadful sadness and grief they were experiencing was to provide them not only with His comforting presence, but also with explanation and understanding. He knew what their greatest need was, and so He walked along with them, teaching and explaining all that was happening to them until they fully understood that God was at the very center of what was occurring.

The sense of intimacy that the disciples experienced on the road to Emmaus was also experienced by David many centuries before. When David continues to write, 'You know when I sit and when I rise; you perceive my thoughts from afar' (Ps. 139:2), he is reminding us that God is fully aware of our every need. Just as Jesus did with those early disciples, God will work in our lives in such a way that we will begin to appreciate His great love for us, His omniscient understanding of us, and His personal and intimate care for us.

In 1984, an American exchange student, whom I subsequently came to know, arrived at Glasgow Bible College one wet morning in early September. Laura Rose had flown across the United States from Portland, Oregon, changed planes in New York, and in the previous twenty-four hours she had successfully traveled the better part of almost 5,000 miles. By the time she arrived, she was very tired and was looking forward to finally getting to the college, meeting the staff, signing the paperwork, and settling into her apartment and going to sleep.

Since she was coming for a year, she brought with her what seemed like the largest suitcase known to humanity. It had four wheels and a length of rope so she could drag it behind her. At the college, she was given keys to her accommodation which was approximately a mile away, and she walked there in the rain.

After climbing the four flights of stairs with her suitcase, she opened the outer door and then the inner door, dropped her case in a nearby bedroom and switched on the light. But nothing happened. She tried again. Still, nothing happened. Then she tried the electric heater in her room, but by now it was clear that there was no power in the apartment. More than a little frustrated, she speculated that the college was not ready for her arrival. 'How could they forget I was coming?' she wondered. She telephoned the college and explained what had happened. A staff member informed Laura Rose that the electrical utilities in student accommodations were operated by a coin meter. This prevents the students from having a large utility bill at the end of each month.

Recognizing her situation, she explained to the college that she had not had an opportunity to change her US dollars into British currency, so the college staff suggested she return to the college where they would exchange some money for her. So Laura Rose closed and locked the inside and outside doors, walked back down four flights of stairs, trudged a mile in the rain, exchanged money and walked back again, eventually arriving in her apartment frustrated, extremely wet, and very tired.

When she put the money into the utilities meter, the power came on. With a sigh of relief, she dropped down on the bed and began to express her frustration. As she prayed, she began to cry, 'Father, why have You brought me thousands of miles from home, to a country where I do not know another living soul, and to a people whose accents I cannot understand? Did I not pray before coming? Did I not ask You to lead and guide me? Did I not trust You in this entire process? Now look at where I am!' There was, however, no immediate answer to her prayer; no comforting sense of affirmation that she was now in the right place; no deep conviction that God had, in fact, directed her to this place. In a mixture of frustration, tiredness, and emotion, she wept for several minutes.

Eventually Laura Rose dried her eyes, went into the bathroom, and washed her hands and face. When she came back to her room she lifted her suitcase onto the bed, unclasped the lock, and lifted the lid. As she lifted the lid, she caught a glimpse of a poster on the wall above the bed that had been left by a student who had graduated the previous year. It was a poster of a mountain range in Portland, Oregon. At the bottom of the poster were these words: 'Grace has brought me safe thus far, and grace will see me home.' Laura Rose sank back onto the bed and wept again, this time for joy. Now she understood in a fresh way the nature of God's leading and guiding. She experienced the reality behind the words of Psalm 139:2: 'You know when I sit and when I rise; you perceive my thoughts from afar.' In the quiet unseen moments of a bedroom in Scotland, thousands of miles from home, His love had washed over her in a new way. Now she finally grasped the truth. He had always been active at the very center of her plans, hopes, and dreams. For months He had been listening to her prayers. He had taken the initiative. He had been leading and guiding her every step of the way.

Ten years after her memorable first day in Glasgow, I met Laura Rose again and reminded her of this story. As I recounted the story she became tearful and said, 'I had forgotten how good God was back then.'

It may be some time since you were reminded of how good God was to you in the past. Perhaps it has been too long since you experienced the thrill and wonder of answered prayer. The freshness, vitality, and sheer invigoration of authentic worship are only distant memories. If that begins to describe you, or if you have never experienced the intimacy of God in the deepest recesses of your heart and mind, come with me further into the wonders of Psalm 139. As you do, my prayer for you is that you will enter into a whole new experience with Him through the pages of His Word. I pray this will be an experience so profound that you will discover a fresh understanding and appreciation of Him who is, 'eternal, infinite, immeasurable, incomprehensible and omnipotent,[4] 'unchangeable in being, wisdom, power, holiness, justice, goodness, love, and truth.'[5] Such an experience may indeed come as a jaw-dropping 'wow' type of surprise, but once you have been surprised by God as He truly is, you will never be satisfied with anything less again.

---

4. James Bulloch, *The Scots Confession a Modern Translation* (Edinburgh, Scotland: Saint Andrew Press, 1991), p. 3.
5. Westminster Shorter Catechism, Answer 4.

Questions

1) Has there been a time in your life when your relationship with God has been particularly close? Explain why.

2) Can you describe a time in your life when God did not immediately answer your prayers? Explain why.

3) Why does David begin this psalm the way he does?

4) Why is worship such a significant part of the Christian life?

5) Why is it helpful to understand that God is the One who takes the initiative in our lives?

6) Is there one thing from verses one and two that stand out to you? Explain why.

2

DISCERNING GOD AT WORK

You discern my going out and my lying down;
you are familiar with all my ways.
Before a word is on my tongue
you know it completely, O LORD.
(Ps. 139:3–4)

Developing Discernment

Like so many others, I receive what feels like a multiplicity of
emails every day. Most are work related, a handful of them are
personal, and occasionally I receive an unforgettable one. Once,
when an unexpected email arrived, I read it several times. I then
read it to my wife. It was the kind of email that you need to read
several times before the enormity of it sinks in. The next day I
posted it on Facebook.

Back in June 2011, my congregation received a visit from
Dr. Tom Marshburn, a NASA astronaut. Tom very kindly
allowed me to briefly introduce him to the congregation, ask
him about his space flights, and how it felt to have had the
experiences unique to an astronaut. We listened intently. Tom's
sister Barbara and her family attend church each Sunday, and

she keeps me up to date with Tom's activities. In 2013 Tom spent almost six months on the International Space Station and on one occasion he sent an email so I could read it to the children at church the following Sunday:

Hi Barbara,

I've written a few sentences for your pastor for this Sunday. Busy days up here—we usually fall asleep in a moment once we get all of our work done and it's bedtime. We have a special place on the International Space Station, a dome formed by seven windows, that is facing the Earth. From this dome we can look 'up' at the Earth 250 miles away and see the ink-black of outer space all around us. We fly in orbit at a speed of five miles per second—think of how fast that is! That's like driving from Greenville to Charleston in forty seconds! And yesterday I watched from this dome of windows as we arced over the Himalayas, tracked down SE Asia, and glided over the emerald blue of the Pacific Ocean. I waited eagerly to see our glorious Sierra Nevada mountain range rising from the horizon to meet us and then glide by below. Next in line was our starkly beautiful SW desert, which melded with the green of the Midwest which in turn folded into the Appalachian Mountains. Just ahead lay the approaching Piedmont plateau, with our green deciduous forests so unique in the world. This trip took just thirty minutes, and all along the way the signs of our existence were tiny and fragile. And at no time did I see any borders made by people like we see on a map, just a constant flow of desert, forest, and ocean. It compels one to give immediate thanks for this brilliant jewel in the universe we call Earth, and to recognize how rare and precious is the gift of our existence.

I think you will agree, receiving an email from the International Space Station is an extraordinary experience and one not easily forgotten! Given the source of this email and the context in which it was written, there is no doubt that we live in a remarkable age. I have read it many times and wondered in utter amazement at the digital sophistication that enabled an email to be sent from space. Barbara also told me on one occasion that her brother Tom called her from space on her cell phone when the entire family was together celebrating their mother's birthday. We truly live in a remarkable age.

Living in a world where much of our leisure time is dominated by smartphones, email, high-tech tablets, social media, and streaming devices, we find that the convenience of a digital playground makes it difficult to slow down enough to find the time to quietly read and reflect on a passage in the Scriptures. Yet, when we do, it is always rewarding.

When David continues by saying, 'You discern my going out and my lying down; you are familiar with all my ways' (Ps. 139:3), he is writing from personal experience. Dr. Charles Swindoll, highly respected pastor and writer, summarizes David's attributes but also his challenges when he writes:

> In many ways he was a most extraordinary man—intelligent, handsome, abundantly gifted as a poet, musician, warrior, and administrator. David had charisma like no Bible character before him to inspire his people and bring his nation to a pinnacle of strength and glory. Yet in other ways he was a most ordinary man—often gripped with destructive passion, rocked by family chaos and personal tragedy, and motivated by political expediency. [1]

As you begin to explore the life of David in the Old Testament books of 1 and 2 Samuel, it is clear that God was preparing this unknown teenager for a relationship with Himself—yet David could not see it coming.

---

1. Charles Swindoll, *David. A Man of Passion and Destiny* (Dallas, Texas: Word, 1997), rear dust jacket.

When we first read of David in 1 Samuel 16:1–13, the chapter opens with God instructing Samuel the prophet to travel to Bethlehem and select one of Jesse's sons to be Israel's next king. Wrestling with grief over the spiritual disintegration of Saul, Israel's king, Samuel is initially hesitant yet nevertheless agrees to go. When he arrives and meets Jesse's oldest son Eliab, he is convinced he has found the next king: 'Surely the LORD's anointed stands here before the LORD' (1 Sam. 16:6). But God tells Samuel that Eliab is not the one He has chosen and reminds him, as each of Jesse's sons appears before Samuel, that He has other priorities: *'Man looks at the outward appearance, but the LORD looks at the heart'* (1 Sam. 16:7).

As the narrative unfolds and draws you into all that is going on, you may begin to wonder, 'What is it that God was looking for in a future king of Israel?' It quickly becomes apparent, however, that God was not concerned with whether the individual was tall or short, or had blond hair or dark hair. He was not looking for a popular, winsome individual with years of leadership experience and expertise. God was looking for someone with character, an individual whose heart was completely surrendered to Him, and who was committed to integrity, transparency, loyalty, and faithfulness in his relationship with Him.

As Jesse's sons appear before Samuel, it is clear that none of them is God's choice and Samuel, somewhat perplexed, inquires if Jesse has any other sons. It is not until the end of this process that we eventually meet David. He was the youngest of the brothers, a seemingly insignificant individual, unimportant, so instantly forgettable that his own father does not even think to mention him to Samuel the prophet. That God would select David clearly comes as a surprise to his family and Samuel, but we learn in subsequent chapters that God had been preparing David for this moment for some time.

Throughout the Scriptures, it is clear that godly leadership is birthed in a relationship, and God had been developing His relationship with David for some time. David had spent a long time in the hill country around Bethlehem looking after his father's livestock. It was in those quiet moments of isolation and seclusion that God had been training David. It was there that David learned some of the most significant lessons of his life. In the midst of such experiences, David learned deep contentment in the call of God. The days David had spent by himself—seemingly alone—were, in fact, spent in the presence of God. Those were the days when David learned the importance of coming to a radical and fresh understanding of God Himself. This was when David understood what it meant to be lost in wonder at the immensity of God's love, to be overwhelmed by the majesty of His presence, and astonished by His grace. Those were the days when David not only was growing in his faith and maturing in his relationship with the Lord, but also was being prepared for the man he would become. David was learning that godly leadership begins in a relationship.

During those days, David was also learning the importance and ongoing significance of obedience and faithfulness in the day-to-day tasks which lay before him. In those quiet, unseen moments, David was learning the lessons of living with the seemingly insignificant. Those who turn out to be servant leaders often are unknown, unseen, unappreciated, and unapplauded. David was learning that the menial, insignificant, routine, regular, unexciting tasks of daily life had meaning and value beyond what he first imagined. It was in the unattractive everyday activities of life that God was seeking faithfulness. It was when no one else was around that David revealed responsibility and diligence in the lonely places; it was there that he proved himself capable and trustworthy as he learned the importance of perseverance in the midst of routine. These lessons helped shape his character in such a manner that, years later, he was able to take on the national responsibilities as king of Israel.

During that period David also learned what so many others have come to learn since. When God develops the character of a person He has set His hand upon, He takes His time. He simply keeps working away, changing, refining, molding and fashioning the character, integrity and transparency, and doing so in moments of deep abiding intimacy with David. It was during these moments that David was experiencing the overwhelming, never-ending love of God—a love so rich and soul-transforming that David was learning to refocus and realign his deepest affections while submitting and surrendering to the rule and reign of God in his life. It may well have been that when David was writing, 'You discern my going out and my lying down; you are familiar with all my ways. Before a word is on my tongue you know it completely, O LORD,' he was thinking of those days.

During this period, David's family and friends had no idea what God was doing, and as we saw earlier, Samuel the prophet thought that God had chosen the eldest brother. The great irony of the passage is that David's name is not mentioned until 1 Samuel 16:13, the last verse in this passage. The writer of 1 Samuel is clearly telling us that those closest to David considered him of little significance. Yet as we know, God had other plans, for 'Man looks at the outward appearance, but the LORD looks at the heart' (1 Sam. 16:7).

On the day that David was anointed king of Israel, the nation, the royal court, the senior civil and military leadership, and the tribal and religious councils were focused on Saul the king. But in Bethlehem where no one was looking, God was focused on David, a seemingly insignificant individual whom no one felt was important—no one except God.

When we are tempted to think of ourselves as insignificant with nothing to offer, we must remember that God does not see us that way. Just as He looked at David, He looks at you with infinite love and sees your value and worth as someone made in His image. The Bible is clear that God has a purpose and plan for each life, and He is seeking to shape individuals who are obedient to His call and faithful in their relationship with Him. He is looking to mold individuals of character, faith, and integrity who will seek to persevere in their relationship with Him in the midst of a busy and demanding lifestyle— individuals who long to have a heart after God's own heart.

When David writes, 'You discern my going out and my lying down; you are familiar with all my ways' (Ps. 139:3), he is reflecting not only on his personal experience but, more importantly, on God's radical engagement with him. The day Samuel arrived at David's house was a routine, normal sort of a day. There was no burning bush, no dream the night before, no angelic appearances or predictions, no suggestions that God was at work in an extraordinary manner, and no indication that David's life would never be the same again.

Having focused on God's shaping and fashioning the actions and intent of David's heart in the context of his routine day-to-day activities, it may be worth pausing for a moment and asking a deeper question, a question with profound implications: Do you have the spiritual discernment to recognize when God is at work in your own life? This question, though not always easy to answer, is certainly worth pursuing.

Discerning God at work calls for a skill-set that does not come easily. Prayerful, reflective consideration—of the decisions we make, the people we interact with, the long-term relationships we develop, how we use our time and the deeply held personal hopes and dreams that we have—calls for a constructive preoccupation with God Himself. When David

41

writes of God discerning his 'going out' and 'lying down,' he uses language that suggests movement and journey, the passive and the active, with each activity seen through the lens of the *daily* as well as the *divine*. When you read of the radical nature of God's interaction with David—'You are familiar with all my ways'—you need to ask if you are as familiar with God as He is with you.

Developing and sustaining a growing and thriving relationship with God always begins with moments of great intimacy which are birthed in prayer. It is in those moments when you are open, vulnerable and transparent before God that He begins to shape your heart and rearrange your disordered desires while realigning and refocusing the deepest desires and motivations of your life. When you begin to enter in to that deep, intimate place of prayer and find yourself climbing into the lap of God and resting there, that is the point when you can bring every care and concern, each uncertainty, the fearful 'what ifs,' the toxic, tranquilizing effects of your sin, and the addictive habits that need to change. This is the time to ask those fearless searching questions that lie deep within the soul and then leave each one with Him and trust Him enough to deal with them. After all He discerns your going out and your lying down, He is familiar with all your ways and you can trust Him, utterly and entirely, with every area of your life. He will not let you down.

Discerning God at Work

During his late teenage years when David first began to discern that God was at work in his life, the thrill of the moment must have been so overwhelming that, not only was he impacted and transformed by the love of God, it is easy to imagine that he was also looking forward with great anticipation to all that was to come.

In 1 Samuel chapters 17–24, which focus on the months immediately following David's anointing as Israel's next king, David triumphed spectacularly over Goliath, was elevated to the inner circle of the royal court, achieved a national profile, and grew in popularity with the people of Israel. During this period, David also developed a lasting friendship with the king's son, Jonathan, and married the king's daughter, Michal. Yet for all of the excitement which David was experiencing during his ascendency, there were challenging days as well. King Saul was mentally and emotionally unstable, his life was dominated by anger and suspicion, as he wrestled with paranoia and the corrosive, invasive nature of jealousy. At the beginning of this period, things took a turn for the worst: 'The LORD was with David... and Saul was afraid of him' (1 Sam. 18:12). During this time, Saul sought to kill David—not once but twice. As the narrative unfolds, you cannot help but wonder if Saul saw in David the man he should have been, yet rather than proactively strive to be the man God had called him to be, he believed it would be easier to eradicate David. By the end of chapter 18, it is clear that David was facing a number of significant challenges.

In the chapters that follow, Saul not only seeks to poison the mind of Jonathan toward David, but he also makes a third attempt on David's life, before dispatching a group of assassins to track him down and kill him. During the earliest moments of those dark days, David becomes distraught and appeals to his close friend, Jonathan. You can hear the desperation in his words, 'What have I done? What is my crime? How have I wronged your father?' (1 Sam. 20:1). After he escapes and seeks the comforting and supportive presence of Samuel the prophet, his friend and mentor, he is hunted once again and flees to the city of Gath, hoping he can find refuge there. When we read that David has sought refuge in the city of Gath, we realize things have become extremely bleak for him. Gath is not only the headquarters of the Philistine army, the historical enemy of Israel, but it was also Goliath's hometown. David would, of course, be instantly recognized. He fears for his life once again and very graphically feigns insanity (1 Sam. 21:13).

At this point you might begin to ask yourself with incredible sadness, 'What has happened to David, the one anointed as king? Where was the David who refused to be subdued, coerced or manipulated by Saul and Goliath? What happened to David whose absolute confidence in the living God was unflinching and uncompromising? What was it that had impacted the trust of the shepherd boy who wrote, "The LORD is my Shepherd; I shall not be in want" (Ps. 23:1)?' David is now reduced to deception and pretense, claiming insanity—he has hit rock bottom. When God is radically at work in someone's life, that experience can be, at times, very painful. David, the once-popular national leader, who was self-confident, self-sufficient, and emotionally stable, whose trust and confidence in the living God had been absolute when facing Goliath, was now in a very different place. Emotionally and spiritually fragile, wounded, debilitated, and on the brink of total collapse, he was now in a place so dark, so lonely, and so isolated, it was difficult for him to find even a glimmer of hope.

I imagine David would be distressed and utterly distraught, asking a series of profound questions such as: 'Lord, where are You when I need You? Why are You letting this happen to me? Have I not been faithful to You? Did I not seek to follow You? Did You not have Samuel anoint me as Israel's next king? Why are You not answering my prayers and coming to my rescue? I have lost my position at court and my rank as an army officer.

I am separated from my wife, my friends, and hunted by Saul as an outlaw. Lord, what are You doing?'

As you pause and consider all that David endured, perhaps you have asked similar questions when you have experienced difficult periods in your own life. Often the first question we ask when facing major difficulties is, 'Father, why would You allow this to happen to me?' Yet, what David experiences next is one of God's great compliments, and David could not see it coming. When God is seemingly conspiring against us, we do not always have the spiritual discernment to realize that, despite the pain involved, He is at the very center of it all. Even more significantly, He is maturing us in the process. It is extremely important for us, in the midst of tough days, to remember that Psalm 139:3 has been written from personal experience: 'You discern my going out and my lying down; you are familiar with all my ways.'

A Deeper Intimacy

I have a good friend who is the former United States ambassador to Canada and served from 2005–2009. When I asked him about his period of service, he told me that one of his first duties was to appear before the Canadian Parliament. While on his way to the Parliament in a chauffeured limousine, complete with a police escort, he turned to his wife and asked her, 'Did you ever imagine in your wildest dreams that we would find ourselves in a situation like this?' His wife responded with a smile and said, 'David, you are not in my wildest dreams.' Susan was imagining spending time with her children and grandchildren and wonderfully enjoying those moments, and David did not feature anywhere in her 'wildest dreams.' I have heard my friend tell that story several times and people always respond the same way—they laugh. We tend to think of 'our wildest dreams' as experiences that involve laughter, happiness, and deep contentment, yet the process of fulfilling our wildest dreams in reality can be extremely demanding. They were painful when David was being hunted by Saul; yet, much to his surprise, he discovered that God was working in and through those experiences.

When David writes, 'Before a word is on my tongue you know it completely, O LORD' (Ps. 139:4), he is not writing from a theoretical or hypothetical understanding of God. Once again, he is writing from personal experience. When David's life is spared and he leaves the city of Gath (see 1 Sam. 22), he is a wanted man with Saul's forces pursuing him. When David seeks refuge, solitude, and protection in a cave in the wilderness, much to his surprise and delight, he also discovers a great deal more than he had initially sought. Opening up his heart, David records in Psalm 57 what he was experiencing at the time.

Psalm 57 begins: 'Have mercy upon me, O God, have mercy on me' (v. 1). In these words, we find David coming to the realization that everything he has placed his trust in has been removed. He has nowhere to go and no one to help him. His reputation as a national leader is now gone, his friends and family are no longer able to encourage or support him, and he is a penniless outlaw with nowhere to go. He is understandably fearful for his life. The future holds no potential or promise. So it is from a position of deep despair that David cries out, 'Have mercy on me, O God, have mercy on me.' He is grief-stricken for what was, and heartbroken for what should have been. He is hopeless and desolate, but God has not finished with David.

In Psalm 139, we learned that God knows us more intimately than we know ourselves. He understands us at a level that is exhaustive and complete. When David writes, 'Before a word is on my tongue you know it completely, O LORD' (Ps. 139:4), he is telling his readers that God's knowledge of him was so complete that He was aware of David's greatest need in a way that he, David, was oblivious to. Please understand the significance of what occurs next. His greatest need is not to be restored to his position in the royal court or as a senior military leader. Restoring David's relationships with Jonathan and Samuel, helpful, formative and encouraging as those relationships were, these are not David's greatest need. David's greatest need was for an ever-increasing, relationally rich, deep, dependent intimacy with God Himself. It is when David finally reaches rock bottom that he discovers the wonderful truth of his own words: 'For in you my soul takes refuge' (Ps. 57:1). Now, at last, David has got it. He realizes that placing his confidence and trust in position, wealth, reputation, and relationships will never ultimately satisfy him because God has greater plans for him than he could imagine.

Free from all plans, hopes, and dreams, David reaches a breakthrough moment in his understanding and realization of what God was doing and pours his heart out as he moves to a place of ever-increasing, profound trust. He has begun to engage with the astonishing truth that 'God… fulfills his purpose for me' (Ps. 57:2). David has finally grasped hold of the truth that God has been teaching him during this extremely difficult period. When people place their trust and confidence in the things around them, those things become substitutes for the thrill of a living relationship with God Himself. It is as if God is saying to David, 'As long as you depend on someone else, you will never fully rest in Me. As long as your confidence is in something else, your entire trust will not be in Me. David, positions of influence and authority, fame and reputation, cannot be a substitute for a living, growing relationship with Me. David, I have so many plans for you. These other things cannot give you what I can give you. They cannot take you where I want to take you. They cannot expose you to a new and fresh appreciation of My deep, enduring love and faithfulness. They cannot reveal to you the majesty, power, and glory that are found in Me. They cannot bring the radical surgery required in your life that will reveal in you My refining hand. They cannot birth in you a passionate desire for holiness and a deep longing for My presence. David, My single greatest desire for you is to transform you into a man after My own heart and when your trust, dependency, and focus are on other things, that cannot happen.' At last, David is becoming familiar with the ways of God. Finally, he is beginning to understand that when it feels as if God is conspiring against him, in reality the purposes and plans God has for him are much greater than he could ever imagine.

As David continues to record his experience of God in Psalm 57:3 and the verses which follow, he does so with a fresh understanding and a new appreciation of the purposes of God. The discernment to realize that God is at work has clearly come into focus in the heart of David. Despite all that he has been through, he now recognizes that the faithfulness of God is a direct reflection of His divine nature. Faithfulness is who God is and manifests itself in His refusal to abandon David to his own inadequate understanding of the character and nature of God. God reveals to him that He loves him too much to allow him to continue to limp through life and struggle with the debilitating nature of his own disappointments, overly dependent upon his own resources.

David is now at the point where he no longer needs to place his trust and confidence in anything or anyone else than God. His eyes are now looking up, no longer focused on what is immediately in front of him, but focused on God alone.

As Psalm 57 unfolds, it is clear that God has shaped and fashioned David's life, and a different person has emerged. No longer do we have a man who is searching for refuge in solitude and isolation. Now we see a man who understands that God's seeming rejection is nothing more than His redirection. David no longer looks to the past to determine his future. He has moved on, firmly closing the door on the past, turning the key and throwing it away as he now focuses on the future. His head is up and he is walking tall. He no longer feigns insanity, no longer seeks momentary relief from all he is facing. The temporary and the transient no longer hold appeal. He is no longer dominated by the debilitating nature of feigning insanity, crouching in the darkness, rocking back and forward while focusing on his paralyzing and fearful concerns about the future. The tears and introspection are gone; the ache of a broken heart over what might have been has vanished; energized and inspired, David is once more focused on the living God. At last he has prayerfully begun to surrender to the pervasive presence of the grace of God and is delighted to be overwhelmed by Him once again. He is at last focused on who he is becoming rather than on who he has been.

When he writes, 'My heart is steadfast, O God' (Ps. 57:7), he repeats it a second time revealing his astonishment that he should find himself in such a situation when so recently the opposite had been true. But now after being radically and supernaturally engaged by the living God, David is a different person. As a result, he does what so many of us do when God is at work in our lives—his heart instinctively moves to worship, adoration, and praise: 'I will sing and make music, Awake, my soul! Awake, harp and lyre! I will awaken the dawn' (Ps. 57:8). David's instinctive response to what God is doing is to worship Him with a thankful and grateful heart.

Now we begin to see what God saw when He first chose, called, and anointed David, the young shepherd boy from Bethlehem. 'Man looks at the outward appearance, but the

LORD looks at the heart' (1 Sam. 16:7). In Psalm 57, we catch a glimpse of the very heart of David, that inward place that only God truly sees. He has been brought to the place where God can truly begin to shape him and use him. He is now standing tall, dependent on no one—firmly and confidently placing his trust in God alone.

At the end of all that David experienced, we see a rare combination of courage, resourcefulness, and faith. David exhibited a willingness to look at the future and hand it over entirely to the purposes and plans of God. David had learned to discern when God was at work in his life. He had learned that God knew him absolutely and unconditionally: 'Before a word is on my tongue you know it completely, O LORD' (Ps. 139:4). David had experienced for himself the radical engagement of God. He knew what it meant to be refreshed and renewed in the concentrated brilliance of God's unsurpassed glory. David understood what millions through the centuries have subsequently come to understand. As a direct result of being exposed to the love, grace, and intimacy of God, uncertainty and apathy disappears, while faithfulness is enabled and sustained. Although, at times, difficult and complex circumstances will continue to be part of our lives, they take on much less significance because we no longer focus on the challenges we face, but on God's initiative and response in grace. There would—from time to time—be dark days ahead for David, but it would be many years before he would be this low again.

Questions

1) How often do you take time to spend with God alone? Explain why.

2) Explain the importance of God's words to Samuel, 'Man looks at the outward appearance, but the LORD looks at the heart' (1 Sam. 16:7).

3) Explain why David begins Psalm 57 in the way he does.

4) How do you discern when God is at work in your life?

5) Why does God take David through a time of uncertainty and remove from him so much of what was comfortable and known to him?

6) Can you describe a time when God intentionally led you in a direction which was radically different from what you had first imagined?

3

A RADICAL UNDERSTANDING

You hem me in—behind and before;
you have laid your hand upon me.
Such knowledge is too wonderful for me,
too lofty for me to attain.
(Ps. 139:5–6)

Your DNA

Recently a friend informed me that she had taken a DNA swab from the inside of her dog's cheek, had sent it off for analysis and the results had come back in the mail that morning. When I enquired why she wanted to know the composition of her dog's DNA, she told me that the results would tell her if her dog was part Collie, part Labrador or a purebred. She assured me that this was helpful for both owners and future owners, as Labradors, for example, often make good family pets. They are friendly around children, have a warm temperament, and are good-natured.

The following Sunday, in a moment of unguarded silliness, I mentioned this to my congregation as I was seeking their support for taking DNA swabs of the church elders. The results, I assured them, would tell us if the elders were part Methodist, part Pentecostal, or perhaps they had an Episcopal background with nondenominational tendencies. I was also anticipating that the DNA analyses would tell me whether they were warm individuals, family-friendly, and affectionate with children. On the other hand, the test results might reveal who the pure pedigrees were, who was highly strung, wouldn't cooperate and needed their tummy rubbed, and told what a 'good dog' they were. The congregation so enjoyed my lightheartedness that they eagerly supported my DNA testing idea, especially as I held up a Q-tip, invited the elders to remain after the service, and assured them that it was a painless process.

When David writes, 'You hem me in—behind and before; you have laid your hand upon me. Such knowledge is too wonderful for me, too lofty for me to attain' (Ps. 139:5-6), he is indicating that God not only knows the intricate details of our DNA, but He also seeks to actively engage us in a daily and detailed manner. David is reassuring us that there are no details in our lives that God overlooks as He consistently orchestrates our life circumstances such that His purposes and plans are at times 'too wonderful for me, too lofty for me to attain.' When David writes these words, he once again writes from personal experience.

In 1 Samuel 17, we come across one of the best-known narratives in all of Scripture, the account of David and Goliath. One of the difficulties in knowing a story so well is that we are often tempted to believe that we also know the principles the story teaches. I am convinced that as we examine the record of David and Goliath, however, we will come to a fresh understanding of the lessons David learned from this extraordinary experience.

For the most part, the biblical books of 1 and 2 Samuel relate the historical account of the advent, establishment, and consolidation of the monarchy in Israel. At the beginning of

1 Samuel, the people of Israel were a loosely organized federation of tribes unable to keep neighboring enemies at bay. The Philistines were an aggressive tribal group that occupied parts of southwest Palestine from approximately 1200 to 600 BC. At various times in their nations' two histories, the Philistines and Israelites found themselves at war. The historical context of 1 Samuel 17 reveals Goliath, the Philistine champion, issuing a challenge to Israel's King Saul to either fight or provide a champion to fight on his behalf. By the time David arrived on the scene, the Israelite leadership and armed forces had become infected by a volatile and lethal atmosphere of fear and suspicion.

Wisdom and Self-Control

As you are drawn into the action of 1 Samuel 17 in its historical context, you begin to sense that there is a great deal more going on than you first imagined.

When David, who was probably in his late teens at this time, was sent by his father to bring food supplies to his brothers on the battlefield, Goliath appears and challenges the Israelites to participate in a representative battle—a one-on-one fight to the death. As David watches this unfold, he asks, 'Who is this… that he should defy the armies of the living God?' (1 Sam. 17:26). Yet David's innocent inquiry elicits a surprising response.

David's older brother Eliab burns with anger and asks David, 'Why have you come down here? And with whom did you leave those few sheep in the desert? I know how conceited you are and how wicked your heart is; you came down only to watch the battle' (1 Sam. 17:28). Even at a cursory glance, it is clear that Eliab is angry with David and is deliberately seeking to be dismissive of David in front of others.

Now before we go any further, it is worth remembering that when we first read of Eliab in 1 Samuel 16, Samuel the prophet mistakenly thought that since Eliab was the firstborn in Jesse's family, he must be the one whom God had chosen as Israel's next king. As we now consider Eliab's response to David, we are left wondering if there is some unresolved jealousy toward David festering below the surface in Eliab's life. Does Eliab, like Samuel, think that he should have been anointed as king? Is Eliab quietly questioning all that has taken place?

What does David, the shepherd boy, know about the challenges of national leadership, military strategy, or negotiating with the Philistines? What experience does he have in developing Israel as a nation, or about local, national, and international trade or economic growth? Surely I should have been chosen. I am the firstborn, the oldest. Have I not served my father and my family well over the years? Surely Samuel got this wrong. After all, he is getting old. Perhaps he misinterpreted what God said. I should have been anointed. I know I have a lot to learn, but I am willing to do whatever it takes. Who does David think he is? I should be the king.

The contrast between Eliab and David could not have been greater. Knowing that the charges Eliab levels against him are not true, David wisely does not seek to justify himself or to argue with Eliab. David knows what is going on in his own heart. His only concern is what God thinks of him; what others think is secondary. The temptation to defend himself in front of others and to squabble with his brother, I imagine, was strong, but he refuses to give in to such a temptation. David does, however, respond in a manner typical of a younger brother: 'Now what have I done? Can't I even speak?' (v. 29). Yet having been charged with being conceited and having a wicked heart, David shows considerable wisdom and self-control in refusing to justify himself or take up his brother's challenge.

'Let no one lose heart'

As 1 Samuel 17 develops, Saul, the king, hears about David's response to the threat of Goliath and sends for David. Saul is well aware of what has taken place over the last forty days as Goliath has dominated the battlefield and humiliated not only Saul, but also the people of Israel. Goliath is nine feet tall, striking in appearance, physically strong, athletic, intimidating, and formidable. As the Philistines' champion, he also has an impressive track record of success when it comes to individual combat.

In 1 Samuel 16, which we looked at in chapter two, Samuel the prophet was looking to anoint a new king, and David's family believed him to be ineligible as they considered him to be insignificant. Yet when Samuel interacted with David and his family, he learned a foundational principle: 'Man looks at the outward appearance, but the LORD looks at the heart' (1 Sam. 16:7). The same principle also applies here. David's brothers, Saul, and the entire Israelite army are fully focused on Goliath's external appearance, his record as a champion, and his intimidating presence. It could be said that Israel's leaders were allowing Goliath to determine the conditions of the battle, and, in so doing, were allowing fear, intimidation, and uncertainty to dominate their thinking and their response.

We also need to notice that there is an important spiritual lesson to be learned here. The moment we permit a perceived threat to dictate how we think, or allow it to influence and shape our response to the challenge before us, we are on our way to compromise and defeat. I must repeat this principle: *the moment we permit a threat to dictate how we think, or to influence and shape our response, we are on our way to compromise and defeat.* David utterly refuses to accept that Goliath is the overwhelming threat he seems to be. David determines that Goliath will not intimidate or coerce him into surrender. He rejects wholesale the enormity of the threat Goliath is presenting and says, 'Let no one lose heart on account of this Philistine; your servant will go and fight him' (1 Sam. 17:32).

For the past few years, David has been immersed in the intimacy, immediacy, and the immensity of God. He has learned the importance of standing strong and trusting in the invincibility and invisibility of God's grace. The many hours that he has spent in the daily routine and dull monotony of looking after his father's sheep have taught him that, when the sheep are threatened and attacked by wild animals, and even when his own life is under threat, God can be trusted in the most difficult of circumstances.

When God chose David, He was not looking for charisma. God was looking for character. David had learned that the menial, unexciting tasks of daily living were important. The routine and seemingly insignificant have meaning and value far beyond the everyday. The everyday activities of demonstrating responsibility, diligence, and faithfulness have created within David the strength of character he now needs when facing Goliath. In the midst of the mundane and the daily, a maturing process has taken place in the life of David as God has refined and fashioned him after His own heart. He is learning that deep and lasting contentment are found in his relationship with the living God. The priorities in David's life are clear. God dominates David's life and thinking, not Goliath. David knows he does not have to cower in fear before Goliath because he knows that, whatever the challenges, God is faithful. David knows that the same God who has answered his prayers in the past, the One who told Samuel to anoint him as king when so many others considered him insignificant, would not abandon him now. David knows from personal experience that God is sufficient for the challenges that lie before him. The reality of this truth is reflected in David's own words, 'You have laid your hand upon me, such knowledge is too wonderful for me, too lofty for me to attain.' The faithfulness of God has been the source of immense value to so many down through the centuries since the time of David, and prompts within us this question when we are facing a significant challenge: 'Is God sufficient for the challenge that lies before me?' For David, and for us, the answer is a resounding *Yes*.

King Saul, for his part, initially resists David's offer to face Goliath, yet after listening to his reasoning and profound confidence in God's ability to deliver him, Saul offers David the only protection he can: his armor. David attempts to function in Saul's armor and discovers fairly quickly that it will not help him, and suspects it will become a burden to him. He cannot face intimidation, fear, and aggression while pretending to be someone he is not. David is aware that transparency, authenticity, and integrity are paramount, and he must be free from the clutter of pretending to be someone else. He is firmly convinced that God has prepared him for what is coming, and he will not deceive himself into thinking he can handle it in his own strength. David's focus is not on himself, and neither is it on Saul, Goliath, or anyone else. David's approach is to focus intentionally on the living God, which in turn enables him to perceive what others cannot.

The spiritual discernment to sense God at work in the midst of a major challenge does not come easily. It is something we need to cultivate and nurture. David was neither intimidated by nor impressed with Goliath. No matter how powerful Goliath appeared to be, David would not give in to the temptation to surrender or compromise. He knew God to be more powerful and more impressive than Goliath could ever be. David was determined to remain faithful to the life God had called him to, and he understood he needed to take a stand. David's relationship with God enabled him to respond in a manner which many others have learned since—to do the natural things spiritually and the spiritual things naturally.

Surprise! Surprise!

There are, for most of us, moments when we find ourselves not only surprised at the circumstances that lie before us, but also a little uncertain about how we should respond. Sometimes surprises are welcome, like an unexpected promotion at work or a salary increase. Or we may discover that after dating for some time, we have fallen in love and had not initially seen it coming. Other kinds of surprises, however, are not so enjoyable. How do you respond when you lose the job you really enjoyed and hoped to make it your career? How do you respond when a friendship you treasured has turned sour, and the person you believed to be a friend is not the person you thought? What do you do when your long-desired hopes and dreams do not become a reality? What do you do when there are tensions and unresolved difficulties in your family? How do you respond to an overwhelming challenge that you did not anticipate?

When David eventually appears before Goliath, he comes face to face with the most difficult challenge of his life so far, and quickly realizes that action is required if Goliath is to be defeated. There may be times in your own life when you are facing a major problem, and you begin to realize that you have to take action as no one else will take action for you—not a counselor, not a parent, not a friend. Facing up to the major challenges in your life can be a lonely and discouraging business, yet when you face up to those challenges, recognize them for what they are, and firmly stand against them, God is often maturing you in the process. Such an experience enables you to grow in your faith and often compels you to live in a place of profound trust—not a casual, nonchalant trust, but a deep, heartfelt, dependent trust in God, and in Him alone. Genuine trust in the midst of an overwhelming threat often blossoms into grappling with a foundational biblical principle. If you try to face an overwhelming challenge in your own strength, you will inevitably fail.

Pause and Consider

Before we explore how David responded to the threat of Goliath, I would like to pause and take you on a brief detour that I think you will find helpful as I am seeking to examine the single greatest challenge to growth in the Christian life. The question which lies at the heart of this challenge involves your asking, 'Why do we continue to sin while seeking to live a Christlike life?' In order to honestly face up to the reality of this question, we need to examine what sin is and the powerful impact it has on our lives. The next few paragraphs are not for the fainthearted, but please persevere. It is essential that you understand this foundational biblical truth.

One Sunday morning some time ago, I was involved in exploring with my congregation *The Apostles' Creed*. When we came to the stanza, 'I believe... in the forgiveness of sins,' we examined in detail the impact and consequence that sin has on our lives. In wrestling through a biblical understanding of what sin is and its innate power to damage and debilitate what it comes in contact with, we were surprised to discover that recognizing sin for what it is—and how to resist it—was a cathartic and emancipating experience.

In the weeks leading up to our exploring *The Apostles' Creed*, one hundred and forty people were killed in suicide bombs and terror attacks in Iraq. A two-year-old girl was shot in the head while sitting in a car seat as two men argued in her home nearby. A St. Louis man was arrested for pouring gasoline on his girlfriend and setting her on fire. She was taken to the hospital in critical condition. In Orlando, Omar Mateen murdered forty-nine people, injured fifty-three more, and was so calm that he called the police in the middle of the massacre to report what he was doing. In Dallas, Texas, five police officers were killed while on duty at a protest rally. In Nice, France, eighty people were killed when a truck mounted the sidewalk and ran them over. Sadly, we live in a world where people are being shot in nightclubs, shopping malls, and high schools, where car bombs and suicide bombs kill, maim, and destroy in acts of senseless violence.

When the Bible talks about sin and its horrific effect on humanity, it describes sin as ugly, dark, distasteful, and utterly shocking. We see the horror of sin manifest itself in a multiplicity of ways including human trafficking, domestic violence, child abuse, and alcohol and drug addiction. Sin brings pain, grief, and trauma so debilitating that many people never fully recover.

The Bible describes sin in language that is stark and austere. It does so because sin by its very nature is deceptive, enticing, enslaving, and addictive. Jesus describes sin as being so powerful that it not only brings spiritual blindness (Matt. 15:14; 23:26), but also influences those it comes into contact with in a manner so radical that they become spiritually lost. 'For the Son of Man came to seek and to save what was lost' (Luke 19:10). The apostle Paul, using equally strong language to describe sin, reminds his readers that sin is so potent, so utterly destructive, that it brings about spiritual death, and that only a transformative relationship with Christ brings spiritual life. 'As for you, you were dead in your transgressions and sins.... But because of his great love for us, God, who is rich in mercy, made us alive with Christ even when we were dead in transgressions' (Eph. 2:1; 4-5).

In writing his Gospel, the apostle John, after years of reflecting on the life of Christ and the effect of sin on humanity, compellingly reminds his readers that '[l]ight has come into the world, but men loved darkness instead of light because their deeds were evil. Everyone who does evil hates the light, and will not come into the light for fear that his deeds will be exposed' (John 3:19-20). Although the Bible describes sin in terms of how it impacts us (i.e., without Christ in our lives we are spiritually lost, blind, and dead), it goes on to remind us that this is not the whole truth. The central truth of the Bible is that the gospel is able to transform our hearts and souls and bring us into an intimate relationship with Christ—and this utterly emancipates us from the tranquilizing, deceptive, enticing, enslaving, addictive power of sin. When Jesus said, 'You will know the truth and the truth will set you free' (John 8:32), He was describing the experience of millions of people down through the centuries when they surrender to the call of the gospel.

Emancipated from the all-pervasive, dominant power of sin, the Christian experiences the wonder and joy of living a life set free by the love and enabling grace of God at a level it is hard to imagine until we surrender to the call of God upon our lives. To move from spiritual death to life, from darkness to light, from a distant and uncertain relationship with Christ to one overwhelmed and transformed by His love—is what takes place when an individual surrenders and then submits to the call of God. Knowing, enjoying, and profoundly trusting in the unmerited love of God is why David was able to write, 'You hem me in—behind and before; you have laid your hand upon me. Such knowledge is too wonderful for me, too lofty for me to attain' (Ps. 139:5-6).

Open and Honest

Having described the power and the impact that sin has on our lives, and also the transforming and emancipating power of the gospel, I wonder if you have been a little uncomfortable reading this chapter—uncomfortable in the sense that, although you may have a living relationship with Christ, you would be open and honest enough to say that you wrestle and struggle with sin and are not growing in your faith the way you would like. In fact, if you and I were sitting down with a cup of coffee and the conversation moved to a deeper level, you may be honest enough to admit that you are struggling in your faith.

If I were to ask you to explain a little about why you are struggling, you may confess there is one particular area in your life that you have never shared with anyone as it causes you to sin, and to sin badly. Yet you have tried, and tried, and tried, and, quite honestly, after failing so often, you have given up. When that particular temptation enters your mind, you cannot seem to resist it. You have tried to resist it, but now if you are being fearlessly honest, you have stopped resisting. You have a relationship with Christ and you know what the Scriptures teach about the power of the gospel to conquer sin, yet you cannot shake off this particular sin. You may have tried for years, yet you continue to fail, and fail badly. You have even tried to ignore it, and now you have settled for learning to live with it. For you, the question uppermost in your mind is, 'How do I defeat this sin? What can I do?' Perhaps you would even say, 'I feel so helpless that I have become a slave to it.' You could easily describe this sin as your greatest single challenge. Could it be that this is your 'Goliath'? In order for you to defeat this sin and have victory over it, there are two biblical principles you need to grasp and then put into action. Please be patient, however, as I try to make one final point before we look at the solution to tackling a persistent sin.

The remarkable growth of social network sites Facebook and Twitter have led sociologists and psychologists to suggest that this unprecedented growth in social media is a desire for connectedness and intimacy birthed in a longing for relationship, identity, and community. In terms of personal relationships, we recognize that being disconnected can lead to being dysfunctional. People raised in difficult family situations with very little love and care often find themselves caught in a trap of insecurity and confusion. This, in turn, leads to being relationally dysfunctional because those involved have been disconnected from a wholesome and healthy family environment. Connectedness and intimacy are essential for growth and development within a family.

Immediately prior to facing up to the challenge of Goliath, David has been enjoying days of incredible intimacy with God—days which have been quiet and restful, days of renewal and refreshment, days when he has been connected with and resting in the presence of God. The lesson here is clear. When we are consistently wrestling with and failing to overcome sin in our own lives, it often occurs when we are not daily connecting with God in a deep and intimate manner—spending time with Him, being strengthened by Him, being refreshed and renewed in Him. Open, honest, intimate, consistent engagement with God on a daily basis is the first critical principle we need to learn and then apply.

The second principle is more complicated but is crucial if we are ever to recognize and then defeat persistent sin. Some time ago I listened to a colleague in ministry explain what he called the 'Temptation Cycle.' I found it so helpful I have tried to apply it since then. The temptation cycle involves several stages. It initially begins with deception, followed by attraction, which leads to preoccupation, and finally conception. The New Testament epistle of James helpfully highlights what is involved when he writes, ' When tempted, no one should say, "God is tempting me." For God cannot be tempted by evil, nor does he tempt anyone; but each person is tempted when they are dragged away by their own evil desire and enticed. Then, after desire has conceived, it gives birth to sin; and sin, when it is full-grown, gives birth to death' (James 1:13-15).

As a pastor, I occasionally find myself in a situation when someone comes to see me and confides in me, admitting to an extramarital affair. After explaining what has taken place, the person will inevitably add, 'I don't know what I was thinking. I have lost my mind. How could I have possibly done this? What was I thinking?' But sadly the person involved is usually not thinking. When an affair takes place, the wronged spouse often experiences devastation, abandonment, self-doubt, loss of self-esteem, insecurity, feelings of deficiency, worthlessness, and is deeply traumatized by an overwhelming sense of betrayal. When children are involved, they are often left feeling insignificant, discarded, and somehow to blame.

When the truth of what has taken place is finally recognized, those involved often look back and realize they have been deceived. The intoxicating and tranquilizing power of illicit passion reminds us once again that sin at its core is deceptive, enticing, enslaving, and addictive.

When the Bible describes the deceptive nature of sin and warns us to be extremely careful when we are initially tempted, it is reminding us that the number one goal of temptation is deception. In the earliest moments of temptation, sin's initial goal is to reassure you that what you are doing or thinking about doing is really not a big deal. Sin convinces us that it is nowhere near as serious as you think it is. After all, everyone thinks and acts this way. It is entirely natural.

To complicate matters further, deception quickly moves us to the next stage which strengthens deception with a powerful sense of attraction. The source of our temptation not only deceives us, but is also alluring, enticing, and attractive. It makes us feel good. It brings us pleasure. It can be from something as seemingly innocuous as gossiping all the way through to drug or alcohol addiction. When we find ourselves gossiping, for example, we have information that other people don't have. We know something they don't and, before we recognize it for what it is, we have become the center of attention. We have an audience. Others are paying attention. We have something other people want. The focus is on us. We know something they don't. We are tempted to say to ourselves, 'I believe that this information belongs to me, it is mine, that I should feed it and nourish it. It is "my precious".' But in the process, before we know it, we have assassinated someone's character; we have taken that person down in order to build ourselves up. Sin is deeply deceptive while being very attractive.

When you wrestle with the addictive nature of sin it often begins with the harmless thought, 'Surely this can't harm anyone, and, after all, I can control it.' In those early moments of temptation, sin seems so attractive. Yet it is also so addictive, and just the thought of it brings pleasure and fulfillment. We tend to forget that there is within temptation an enslaving addiction that is overwhelming. It tends to lead to an uncontrollable preoccupation, complete with cravings and compulsions that cannot be easily shaken off. When deception gives birth to attraction, (which in turn grows into addiction, followed by preoccupation and finally conception), we lose the ability to exercise good judgment. We can no longer control our behavior and it draws us into a self-destructive, debilitating pattern that all too often alienates those we love and leaves us isolated, helpless, and ashamed. Sin consistently promises to be exciting, fulfilling, and utterly liberating, yet in reality it is deceptive, enslaving, and addictive. That is why when sin is recognized for what it is, we say, 'I don't know what I was doing. What on earth was I thinking?'

'You have laid your hand upon me'

When David writes, 'You hem me in—behind and before; you have laid your hand upon me. Such knowledge is too wonderful for me, too lofty for me to attain' (Psalm 139:5-6), he is reminding his readers in a powerful and pertinent way that whatever the enormity of the challenges which lie before them, they never have to face those challenges alone.

So David, who was considered seemingly insignificant and instantly forgettable by his family, utterly refused to be intimidated into surrender, or to allow the threat he faced to influence how he responded to Goliath. David was able to do this because he realized that, in the midst of the challenges he faced, God was with him. God had hemmed him in. Not only had God brought David into a personal relationship of deep and abiding intimacy, there was also never a single moment when David was without the leading, directing, and protecting hand of God. David was innately aware of the call of God on his life and he was utterly convinced that God does not call the enabled, but He enables the called.

It was not the circumstances of his life that had brought David to stand before Goliath. He was not facing Goliath because of poor choices or bad decisions. Rather, he faced Goliath because God had been actively at work in his life and had been preparing him for his greatest challenge. While everyone else was focused on Goliath, David was focused on God. 'You hem me in—behind and before; you have laid your hand upon me' (v. 5). David absolutely refused to focus only on the challenge he faced, but rather he focused on God's resources and strength in grace.

Some time ago, I learned an important lesson from a colleague who talked about the supernatural nature of the sustaining grace of God. He began by challenging those of us who were present to consider 'How many push-ups can you do?' Most of us responded that we were uncertain but we would be willing to try and find out. He then suggested that most of us would begin with determination and commitment. But after a while we would become tired, our muscles would become weak, our arms would begin to tremble, and we would realize that we could only do one or two more before we had to stop. But he went on to suggest that if he offered us a million dollars if we could complete one more push up, we agreed that most of us would try. Finally, he suggested that he would give each of us five million dollars if we could do another ten. In light of what had already taken place we agreed that our response would be 'I can't.' He then went on to prove his point by reminding us that when we try to overcome a major obstacle in our own strength we will inevitably fail, but when we are dependent on God alone and submit and surrender the situation to Him, we can overcome.

Whenever we find ourselves consistently defeated because of the deceptive, enticing, enslaving nature of sin, please understand that God does not expect us to conquer it in our own strength. God did not expect David to defeat Goliath in his own strength. David recognized this, and that is why he was able to say, 'You have laid your hand upon me.'

Today we have a huge advantage over David. When the Holy Spirit came down at Pentecost, as recorded in the New Testament book of Acts, chapter two, those present experienced His indwelling, transforming, enabling power for the first time. From that point on, all who have surrendered their lives to Christ and trusted Him for their salvation moved to a position of profound dependency on the indwelling power of the Holy Spirit. They experienced the Spirit of God at a level they previously did not know was possible. Throughout the New Testament, we are reminded that the same moral and supernatural power that raised Jesus from the dead now lives in us. When we are faced with a besetting sin or an overwhelming challenge, we are called to recognize it for what it is and to hand it over to God, recognizing that we cannot deal with it in our own strength, but that by being utterly dependent upon Him, He handles it for us. The apostle Paul provides a powerful reminder of this principle when he writes, 'No temptation has seized you except what is common to man. And God is faithful; he will not let you be tempted beyond what you can bear. But when you are tempted, he will also provide a way out so that you can stand up under it' (1 Cor. 10:13).

The challenges you face may be found in a variety of places: your job, a family member, a roommate, a lawsuit, health issues, or perhaps an addiction. The fears involved in tackling such a challenge rob you of your energy and seek to drain away your confidence and faith. David learned at a young age that victory was possible when profound trust was placed in God alone. David's reminder that the hand of God has been placed upon us brings incredible peace and confidence. Such truth enables and sustains us and allows us to hand over to Him all that we face, knowing that fear, intimidation, and acceptance of defeat are not the way to live. Compromise and surrender do not lead us to victory and maturity. Learning to stand against the issues we consistently struggle with while placing our trust and hope in the living God does.

This is the truth that lies at the heart of the gospel. Consistently living for Christ, utterly depending on Him, brings real hope along with genuine, credible, authentic change—change that transforms the soul and allows us to live the life God intended, free from the intimidation of sin and the fear of failure.

When David faced Goliath, he did not do so alone. The transforming love and intimate, enabling grace of God strengthened him for what he was facing. He seemed to stand alone, but that was simply not true. He had five smooth stones; it wasn't much, but it was enough. To those watching, David was among the seemingly insignificant and the instantly forgettable. No one thought him capable. Yet he knew he did not have to wrestle and struggle in his own strength, for his confidence was in God alone.

If you are struggling and discouraged, you may be sure that God is there for you. If you are deeply disappointed and hurt over the circumstances of your life, He is there for you. If you are consistently defeated and ashamed at your own sin, He is only a prayer away. He is willing to walk alongside you and bring you forgiveness, strength, hope, and a fresh beginning. God delights in doing the improbable and the miraculous.

When David writes, 'You hem me in—behind and before; you have laid your hand upon me. Such knowledge is too wonderful for me, too lofty for me to attain,' he is writing from personal experience. Such an experience can also be a reality for you.

Questions

1) Describe a time when you struggled with consistently living the Christian life and explain why this was so. Mention one or two things that happened that enabled you to overcome the pattern.

2) When his brother Eliab challenged David, calling him 'conceited' and 'wicked,' David refused to respond to him in an aggressive manner. Explain why this was so.

3) Explain why sin is so powerful and why we so often give in to it. Mention two or three specific examples that come to mind.

4) Explain why David refused to be intimidated by Goliath, and then recount a time when God enabled you to face up to a particular challenge in your own life. What principles applied in David's situation and in your situation? How might you (with greater maturity) now respond to a similar circumstance?

5) What resources does God provide for us when we seek to live for Him on a day-by-day basis?

6) Which part of Psalm 139:5-6 has the most meaning for you? Why? *You hem me in—behind and before; you have laid your hand upon me. Such knowledge is too wonderful for me, too lofty for me to attain.*

4

ENCOUNTERING THE HOLY SPIRIT

Where can I go from your Spirit?
Where can I flee from your presence?
If I go up to the heavens, you are there;
if I make my bed in the depths, you are there.
If I rise on the wings of the dawn,
if I settle on the far side of the sea,
even there your hand will guide me,
your right hand will hold me fast.
(Ps. 139:7–10)

Fearing the What?

Recently I received an email I found hilarious, but, sadly, those I shared it with groaned audibly. 'I know I should be able to get over my phobia of German sausages, but I fear the wurst.' Now I fully appreciate that not everyone has the same sense of humor, but the email was funny and incorporated a clever example of paraprosdokian speech. Paraprosdokian speech is, as you no doubt know, a figure of speech in which the end of a sentence is surprising or unexpected, often causing the reader to reframe or reinterpret the first part.

As we continue to explore the hidden depths of Psalm 139, don't be surprised if you find yourself reframing or reinterpreting your understanding of Psalm 139 and, more importantly, exploring new levels of intimacy in your relationship with God.

This often happens when we intentionally commit ourselves to asking fearless, searching questions about living out our faith in the messiness and distraction of everyday life.

Most of us would agree that life at times is busy, often dominated by a mild addiction to an image-rich, digitally hungry playground where meaning and purpose are determined by how connected we are to the ubiquitous convenience of smartphones and a digitally dependent life. In previous chapters, I mentioned that the immense popularity of social network sites reveals to us that connectedness and intimacy are priorities for all of us. Yet the deeper question to ask is this: Can we truly have connectedness and intimacy with each of our 1,853 friends on Facebook or all of the 1,169 followers on our Twitter account? The perceived need for connectedness and intimacy is clear, but is there depth to those relationships, or are we seeking intimacy through anonymity? For all of the technological sophistication available to us, we are deeply aware that there is so much more to life than a digital existence. A growing, maturing, intimate relationship with God can never be based on a casual connectedness or an insipid intimacy.

When David writes, 'Where can I go from your Spirit? Where can I flee from your presence?' he is asking deep and probing questions—questions that may draw us into a fresh understanding of the nature and character of God; questions that enlarge the mind and warm the heart; questions that take us to a place that is not for the fainthearted, but rather is deeply transformative, a place where the Spirit of God instills within us a passionate hunger to know Him in a deeper, richer, fuller way.

'Where Can I go from Your Spirit?'

When we begin to focus on the questions, 'Where can I go from your Spirit? Where can I flee from your presence?' we immediately wonder why David would want to flee from the presence of God. Why would he wish to escape from the Spirit of God? Is he building on the significance of the truths expressed in the passage immediately before this one? 'You hem me in—behind and before; you have laid your hand upon me. Such knowledge is too wonderful for me, too lofty for me to attain' (Ps. 139:5-6). Are these questions little more than an academic exercise in considering the attributes or characteristics of God's nature expressed in His omnipotence, omniscience, and omnipresence? Or could it be that David is asking these questions as a devotional expression of wonder and incredulity as he considers the joy and the thrill of knowing and worshiping God in His transcendent majesty? Perhaps there is another reason for these questions.

One of the telltale signs of genuine engagement with God is when an individual has a profound encounter with Him resulting in a solemn and sobering realization of the magnitude, significance, and gravitas of his or her sin. Having explored this in a limited sense toward the end of the previous chapter, we are now going a little deeper, but not with David. Surprisingly, we are looking at another individual who sought to escape the deep-seated conviction that encountering the presence of God inevitably brings.

Encountering God in Surprising Places

In the Gospel of Luke, we come across a fascinating incident in which another well-known biblical character whose surprising encounter with Jesus causes him to reframe and reinterpret his relationship with God in a radical manner. When Jesus calls

His disciples, Simon Peter encounters Christ in a way that will have a profound effect on him for the rest of his life.

If I were to ask which individuals in the Bible you most readily identify with, I suspect that somewhere on that list would be Simon Peter. Peter goes through trials and difficulties we can identify with. He grows in stages we can understand. He has an unpredictable nature and is at times rash and impulsive. Yet, like so many others who encounter Christ, he finds his own life wonderfully changed as he becomes one of Jesus' closest friends.

As you begin to read through the early chapters of Luke's Gospel, you realize that a great deal has happened by the time you get to Luke 5:1-11. In those chapters there is a considerable amount of gossip, rumour, and speculation surrounding who Jesus is, and why He was able to conduct the miracles that have impacted so many. This backdrop—which helps us understand the overall context of chapter five—also explains why so many people have gathered to listen to Jesus and why He got into one of the boats in order to speak to the large crowd which had gathered.

When Jesus initially engages with Peter, He does so in the midst of Peter's daily routine. Peter has been out fishing all night, catching nothing; he is now preparing his nets for the next night, when Jesus surprisingly asks Peter if He may use his boat. As Jesus interacts with Peter, what is about to take place comes as such a surprise. I do not imagine that Peter could have anticipated encountering God that morning, yet encounter God he does. In the midst of all that is about to take place, Peter is to discover that God often begins to impact a life in small and seemingly insignificant ways. Jesus' seemingly innocent request on an ordinary workday leads to a profound impact on Peter's life.

When Jesus has finished speaking to the large crowd, He instructs Peter to move his boat out into deep water and let down his nets for a catch of fish. Initially reluctant to do so you can imagine Peter thinking to himself, 'Why would I do this? The daytime is not the right time to catch the fish; that is why we have been fishing all night.' After all Peter is the fisherman and he knows these waters well; yet when he follows Jesus' instructions, Peter is astonished to discover that his nets have become so full that they almost break. It is at this point that Peter, despite his incredulity, realizes what is really going on. Peter, the professional fisherman who has fished the waters of the Sea of Galilee for years and never had such an experience, now begins to understand that Jesus is not simply a wandering rabbi with an engaging ability to communicate. Witnessing for himself the miraculous catch of fish and grasping the unprecedented enormity of what has taken place, Peter now sees Jesus in an entirely different way. He fully realizes that the God of all creation is standing before him and He has orchestrated and engineered the fish to swim into the net. The realization of who Jesus truly is moves Peter to a depth of understanding he could not have previously imagined. His supernatural encounter with Jesus reveals to him in a deeply moving, life-transforming manner, the overwhelming majesty and glory of God Himself. Yet such an understanding also moves him to see himself in a different light as well.

At a cursory glance, Peter's response to Jesus seems strange and out of place. It suggests that he is uncomfortable and distressed with what has just happened, and you immediately ask yourself, why does he cry out, 'Go away from me, Lord; I am a sinful man'? Why is this Peter's instinctive response? Should he not be marveling at the huge quantity of fish or seeking help to land the catch?

When the Spirit of God impacts your life in such an intense manner, two things happen. First, you come to a new understanding and appreciation of the holiness, grace and grandeur of God Himself. Second, you become deeply convicted of your own sin. To encounter God at this level is an unsettling and unnerving experience. When Jesus impacts Peter's life, he realizes in an instant his own unworthiness and wants to flee from the presence of a holy, perfect, sinless God. The fearless, penetrating, all-pervasive light of the love of God illuminates the deepest and darkest recesses of Peter's heart, and brings with it an accompanying sense of conviction that has moved him to the very core of his being. In this experience Peter has an encounter with God that he did not anticipate. Such an experience can be a paralyzing and unnerving encounter.

When an individual becomes aware of the magnitude, gravitas, and significance of his own sin, it is a somber and sobering experience. Yet the Scriptures also teach us that such an experience is often accompanied by an overwhelming awareness of the magnitude, gravitas, and significance of the love and forgiveness of God. When Peter encounters Jesus as He truly is, he cannot remain the man he once was. In recognizing the momentous significance of what Peter is experiencing, Jesus says to him, 'Don't be afraid,' as He is eager for him to understand that encountering the presence of God at a deep and intimate level not only convicts us of our sin, but it also drives us into the joy and deep contentment of encountering His Spirit.

The Role of the Holy Spirit

Have you ever found yourself in the garage looking around at storage boxes, tools, garden equipment, and spare tins of paint, asking yourself, 'Do I really need all this stuff?' This usually happens when you realize it is time to declutter the garage in order to make room for your car. If you have ever needed to clean out your garage or declutter the cupboards and attic in your home, you know it can be a long, painful, complicated experience. It is often painful because you have to make a number of decisions you would rather not make. Those decisions involve asking, 'Will I need this in future?'

A local moving company in my hometown assists individuals and families with the decluttering process as they pack up their belongings to move. This company works closely with you on everything from furniture to clothes to dishes and everything in between. This company is so good that it has female staff members who will help you declutter your wardrobe by gently but firmly asking, 'Do you really need this? Will you ever wear it again?' They may even be so bold as to suggest that a garment is dated or no longer looks good on you. This moving company specializes in helping you make significant and tough decisions that enable you to declutter your 'stuff,' prioritize your life, and move you toward a healthier lifestyle.

Now imagine what it would be like if you had someone who could do that in your soul!

When David was asking, 'Where can I go from your Spirit? Where can I flee from your presence?' he was asking deep and probing questions about the presence and power of the Holy Spirit at work in his life. David's questions and emphasis reflect the parallelism so often used in Hebrew poetry, expressing similar thoughts in parallel words: 'Where can I go from your Spirit? Where can I flee from your presence? If I go up to the heavens, you are there; if I make my bed in the depths, you are there. If I rise on the wings of the dawn, if I settle on the far side of the sea, even there your hand will guide me, your right hand will hold me fast' (Psalm 139:7-10). In asking similar questions in a variety of ways, he is encouraging his readers to come to the clear conclusion that there is nowhere that the Spirit of God cannot reach and refine him.

Throughout the Old Testament, we see the Holy Spirit enabling or anointing individuals to fulfill the purposes of God's redemptive plans. This is seen most clearly in the service of national leaders – prophets, priests, and kings. Yet it would be a mistake to think that the work of the Spirit is restricted or confined to individuals. In the opening verses of Genesis, we find the Holy Spirit playing a central role in the work of creation: 'In the beginning God created the heavens and the earth. Now the earth was formless and empty, darkness was over the surface of the deep, and the Spirit of God was hovering over the waters' (Gen. 1:1-2).

In both Joel (see Joel 2:28–29) and Ezekiel, we find reference to a future outpouring of God's Spirit that involves the indwelling and transforming nature of the work of the Holy Spirit upon all of God's people. 'I will give you a new heart and put a new spirit in you; I will remove from you your heart of stone and give you a heart of flesh. And I will put my Spirit in you and move you to follow my decrees and be careful to keep my laws' (Ezek. 36:26-27).

As we move into the New Testament, we see an important change take place. The emphasis is no longer on the Holy Spirit anointing an individual for a particular period; now it is on the indwelling and equipping nature of the Holy Spirit. 'I will ask the Father, and he will give you another Counselor to be with you forever—the Spirit of truth.... You know him, for he lives with you and will be in you. I will not leave you as orphans; I will come to you' (John 14:16-18). It is also worth noting that Jesus refers to the Holy Spirit as 'He.' The Holy Spirit is not an impersonal force; neither is He simply an influence. He is a person. He teaches, He inspires, He guides, leads, grieves, convicts us of our sin, and refines us in order that we become more Christlike. Moreover, the Holy Spirit is not simply a person; He is also fully divine. The Bible talks about the Christian having a personal relationship with the Holy Spirit just as we have a personal relationship with the Father and with the Son.

The apostle Paul, in describing the work of the Holy Spirit, does so in terms of His work being a distinct and integral feature of the Godhead, thus placing the Holy Spirit on equal footing with the Father and the Son. 'But when the kindness and love of God our Savior appeared, he saved us, not because of righteous things we had done, but because of his mercy. He saved us through the washing of rebirth and renewal by the Holy Spirit, whom he poured out on us generously through Jesus Christ our Savior' (Titus 3:4-6).

Toward the end of the New Testament when Peter focuses on the refining work of the Holy Spirit in our lives, he reminds his readers of the role that each member of the Trinity plays. 'To God's elect... who have been chosen according to the foreknowledge of *God the Father*, through the sanctifying work of *the Spirit*, for obedience to *Jesus Christ* and sprinkling by his blood' (1 Pet. 1:1-2, emphasis added). It is clear from Scripture that there are three distinct Persons within the Godhead, each of whom is understood as distinct and clearly different from the others. Such a distinction must be honored by us—not embraced in a polytheistic sense as several gods—but as one God with three distinct Persons: Father, Son, and Holy Spirit.

When David is anointed at a young age as Israel's next king, the Holy Spirit plays a central role in his anointing and in doing so He equips David for all that is to come. 'And from that day on the Spirit of the Lord came upon David in power' (1 Sam. 16:13). The power of the Holy Spirit at work in David's life convicted him deeply and began a refining process that would last a lifetime, taking him to a place where God would describe David as 'a man after my own heart' (Acts 13:22).

The 'Why' of Pentecost

A number of years ago I moved from Inverness, Scotland, along with my wife and son, to Greenville, South Carolina. During our initial visit, my wife Ruth and son Michael were shopping on Main Street. Recognizing the strange accent, one of the shop assistants inquired where they were from. At that point, another customer entered the conversation, expressing delight in hearing an accent she thought she recognized and saying she had good friends who came from Ireland. She then informed Ruth and Michael that 'They sound just like you.' Ruth and Michael smiled politely as the lady, expressing mild incredulity that they were from Scotland, said, 'My friends do sound exactly like you. Are you sure you aren't Irish?' Michael, who was eighteen at the time, told me later that he was so tempted to reply, 'Madam, you are correct. We are Irish and had hoped no one would notice. Please forgive us.' He did, however, restrain himself as Ruth pleasantly attempted to move the conversation on. My point in telling this story is that the lady involved was attempting to do what so many of us do. She was attempting to filter a new experience through a previous experience.

The coming of the Holy Spirit at Pentecost was an unprecedented event in God's redemptive plan. It was an experience so unprecedented and profound that it could not possibly be filtered through any previous experience. In Acts 2:1-41, we see the revealing and unfolding of a new phase in the eternal purposes of God, beginning with one of the most dramatic and exciting events in the Bible and resulting in the extraordinary and miraculous birth of the infant church and the transformation of those who were present.

In order to fully grasp the context for what took place at Pentecost, try to imagine what had taken place in the lives of the disciples during the previous seven weeks. They had seen the arrest, trial, death, resurrection, and ascension of Christ. They had experienced the emotional extremes of grief at the death of Christ, followed by the overwhelming joy of the resurrection, and finally the news that Jesus must depart and be with His Father. I imagine that such news left the disciples feeling grief-stricken and abandoned once again. No more meals together with Jesus; no more discussions beside the Sea of Galilee; no more quiet talks around the fire late at night; and no more shared laughter, or tears, or watching Him handle some difficult and challenging situation. They would no longer hear Him teach or be deeply moved by His prayers. The joy of His presence would be no more. They felt abandoned and deserted.

In an attempt to reassure and comfort the disciples, Jesus had told them, 'Unless I go away, the Counselor will not come to you; but if I go, I will send him to you' (John 16:7). Upon hearing this news, I imagine the apostles wondered how that could be possible. I also suspect they might have struggled with a multitude of questions and emotions, including uncertainty, bewilderment, and fear about the future. Yet unless Christ ascended to be with His Father, the Holy Spirit would not come.

It is much easier to understand the magnitude and importance of the coming of the Holy Spirit at Pentecost, yet miss the significance of Christ's ascension. If that describes you, please be patient with me as we quickly explore why Jesus would say, 'It is for your good that I am going away' (John 16:7). The ascension of Christ concludes Luke's Gospel, begins the book of Acts, is featured in John's Gospel (John 3:13; 6:62; 14:2-4; 16:5-7; 20:17) and other New Testament documents (Eph. 1:20; Heb. 4:14; Heb. 6:20; 1 Pet. 3:21-22). Even though the New Testament writers place an emphasis on the significance of the ascension it is easy to miss its importance as it may be thought of as an interesting yet esoteric exercise that is not particularly relevant to practical Christian living in the twenty-first century.

Strange as it may seem, however, the importance of the ascension is hard to exaggerate, as it opens the door for the coming of the Holy Spirit at Pentecost. While on earth, Jesus inhabited a human body and, because of the limitations of the human body, He could only be in one place at a time. When He was physically present in Nazareth, He was not physically present in Jerusalem. When He was walking beside the Sea of Galilee, He could not be in Jericho eighty miles away.

At the completion of Christ's earthly ministry when He ascended into heaven, He sent the Holy Spirit, who is not limited by human physicality and is therefore entirely capable of being everywhere at the same time. The Holy Spirit could fill, transform, and empower a man in ancient Palestine, a woman in Syria, and yet another in Rome at the heart of the Empire. The same is true today. Christians in Angola and Alaska, the southern tip of Australia and Austria, can all simultaneously experience that same indwelling power and presence of the Holy Spirit.

It is through the indwelling of the Holy Spirit that intimacy with God is birthed. It is through the deep, all-pervasive presence of the Holy Spirit that we experience the incredible, life-transforming love of God, His eternal forgiveness, and His overwhelming, abiding peace. In Ephesians 3:16, a very moving passage of Scripture, the apostle Paul enables his readers to grasp the significance of the indwelling of the power of the Holy Spirit when he moves from explanation and exposition to heartfelt prayer for his readers, praying that they will experience the strengthening in their inner being which comes from the indwelling power of the Holy Spirit. It was the ascension of Christ that triggered the coming of the Holy Spirit at Pentecost which, in turn, brought them to a level of loving intimacy with Christ that they could not have experienced prior to His ascension.

The Power of Pentecost

In his description of Pentecost, Luke includes a number of significant and fascinating details, including 'a sound like a mighty wind,' 'tongues of fire,' and people from a variety of countries hearing the disciples speaking in their native languages. Luke also informs his readers that those who were present and believed were 'filled with the Holy Spirit'—not just particular individuals, not just the apostles, but everyone. 'All of them were filled with the Holy Spirit' (Acts 2:4). The Holy Spirit was now indwelling *everyone* who believed, not just those in positions of national leadership in Israel, prophets, priests, and kings. Furthermore, His indwelling was not on a temporary basis and neither was it restricted to an enabling or anointing experience. The prophecy of Ezekiel was at last coming to fruition: 'I will give you a new heart and put a new spirit in you; I will remove from you your heart of stone and give you a heart of flesh. And I will put my Spirit in you and move you to follow my decrees and be careful to keep my laws' (Ezek. 36:26-27).

When Peter begins to explain to the vast crowd what has happened, he defines what is taking place in terms of God fulfilling His promises contained within the Old Testament book of Joel: 'I will pour out my Spirit on all people' (Joel 2:28). For the first time in history, people from many different nationalities—Parthians, Medes and Elamites, people from Mesopotamia, Judea and Cappadocia, Pontus, Asia, Phrygia and Pamphylia, Egypt, Libya, Crete, Arabia, and Rome—all are experiencing the transforming presence and indwelling power of the Holy Spirit. Peter's powerful explanation to his listeners reveals that God was not pouring out His Spirit grudgingly or hesitantly, but was extravagantly pouring out His love through the indwelling power of His Holy Spirit.

As a direct result of the Holy Spirit coming at Pentecost, humanity's relationship with God changed forever. From Pentecost onward, individuals who respond to the call of the gospel on their lives begin to understand that they no longer have only an intellectual or emotional awareness of the significance of the death and resurrection of Christ. They now experience for themselves what it means to be impacted by the transforming power of the Holy Spirit. They now have what we touched on in an earlier chapter: the same moral and supernatural power which brought Christ back from the dead was now living within them.

When Jesus speaks His last words to His disciples, 'You will receive power when the Holy Spirit comes on you' (Acts 1:8), He is referring to the indwelling power of the Holy Spirit.

The primary work of the Holy Spirit is to initially bring us from spiritual darkness to spiritual life, and having brought us into an intimate relationship with God, He then shapes, fashions, molds, refines, and empowers us to become more like Christ. In so doing, the Holy Spirit powerfully equips us to live for Christ each day. As an integral part of His refining process, the Holy Spirit begins by enabling us to recognize sin in our own lives—sin that restricts us from growing and maturing in our faith. When God begins to work in our lives, He refuses to do so at a superficial or perfunctory level. It may well be that this is what David was expressing when he wrote, 'Where can I go from your Spirit? Where can I flee from your presence? If I go up to the heavens, you are there; if I make my bed in the depths, you are there.'

When God calls us to Himself and reaches deep within us to engage in radical spiritual surgery, He often begins by convicting us of sinful behavior patterns that need to change. Such an experience is deeply uncomfortable and is often accompanied by heartfelt and profound regret. Yet when God is at work within us, He does not simply move us to a point of regret for poor decisions and bad choices. Neither does He move us to experience only remorse. Rather, He brings us to a point of deep, abiding repentance for giving in to the deceptive, seductive, powerful, enticing attraction of sin and the debilitating and destructive forces it brings into our lives.

For all the tears and sense of shame we experience in heartfelt repentance, the Holy Spirit, however, specializes in replacing repentance with a supernatural joy. When we face up to our sin and confess it, repentance and regrets are replaced with joy as the grace of God enables us to understand the refreshing and renewing power of His love. At that moment, we discover we are being renewed by the indwelling refining power of the Holy Spirit and enabled to follow Him at a level we could not previously have envisaged. As a result of being brought into a new relationship with God we increasingly understand that there is never a moment when we are beyond the intimate care and daily reach of the Spirit of God. This is why David, who at times faced overwhelming challenges, both as an individual and as a national leader with a myriad of significant responsibilities, was able to reflect on the faithfulness of God, writing, 'If I go up to the heavens, you are there; if I make my bed in the depths, you are there. If I rise on the wings of the dawn, if I settle on the far side of the sea, even there your hand will guide me, your right hand will hold me fast' (Ps. 139:7-10).

Nurturing a Life in the Spirit

David's sense of the enabling and strengthening presence of the Spirit of God, along with His powerful and sustaining hand upon his life, was not an experience reserved only for David. In the New Testament book of Romans, chapter eight, one of the greatest chapters in all of Scripture, the apostle Paul writes in detail about what is involved in nourishing a lifestyle utterly dependent on the Spirit of God (Rom. 8:5-17).

Earlier I mentioned that, from Pentecost onward, there is no longer only an emotional or intellectual awareness of the death and resurrection of Christ, but also a realization that the same moral and supernatural power which raised Christ from the dead indwells believers today in the person of the Holy Spirit. If we are to nurture and value an ever-increasing awareness of living in dependency on the Spirit of God, one of the lessons we learn fairly quickly is that the Holy Spirit has no interest in a sterile or academic faith, a faith removed and remote from real life. He is interested in a life submitted and surrendered to Him amidst the messiness, mistakes, disappointments, and regrets of life.

The apostle Paul writes, 'Those who live according to the sinful nature have their minds set on what that nature desires; but those who live in accordance with the Spirit have their minds set on what the Spirit desires' (Rom. 8:5). Here Paul is pointedly reminding us that if we are ever to grow in our faith, we must realistically face up to the internal conflicts that exist when we are committed to a lifestyle of growth and holiness. In earlier chapters we have looked at the deceptive, enticing, tranquilizing effect that sin has on our lives and in Romans 8:5 Paul is reminding us of the importance of consistently resisting the appeal of sin and the value of being intentionally focused on what the Spirit desires.

Most of us, if asked, would have to confess that at times we are powerfully tempted to surrender to the sinful impulses that seek to control and dominate our thinking, define who we are, and determine how we act. Yet experience tells us that when we give in to such temptations, we inevitably end up wrestling internally with anguish and turmoil, insecurity, hostility, resentment, and irritability which often overflows and impacts the people around us. In addition, we become stunted in our spiritual growth. Our prayer life becomes less of a priority, moments of deep intimacy with God become less important, and genuine engagement with God becomes difficult amidst the demands of a busy daily schedule. These are the inevitable results of living 'according to the sinful nature.'

But the second part of Romans 8:5 highlights for us a central truth if we are ever to live according to what the Spirit desires. 'But those who live in accordance with the Spirit have their mind set on what the Spirit desires.' Please notice Paul's emphasis on the role the mind plays when we endeavor to live according to the Spirit. It is worth asking yourself if you are prayerfully feeding and nourishing your mind by spending time in God's Word and focusing on Him. How often do you find yourself lost in the immensity of His love and refreshed and renewed in the concentrated brilliance of His glory? It is when you begin to engage the Spirit of God through the reading of His Word that you begin to grasp and grapple with a mature, biblical understanding of the majesty, grace, grandeur, greatness, and radiance of God Himself. That is the moment when you have your mind set on what the Spirit desires. It begins when you are intentional about spending time in the Scriptures, seeking to know God better, and then applying what you learn to every area of your life. When you willingly apply what Scripture says to the messiness, disappointments, and regrets in your life, that is the moment you are 'controlled not by the sinful nature, but by the Spirit.'

Throughout the Bible, we are taught that growth and development in our relationship with God do not come by chance or accident, but are, in fact, the result of a lifestyle choice, a choice that includes a desire and commitment to cultivate and nourish holiness in all aspects of our daily living. An intentional and prayerful approach to time spent with God each day, along with a ruthless and uncompromising approach to dealing with sin, brings the joy and thrill of a growing faith and an ever-increasing intimacy with God. When you are committed to these lifestyle choices you find that you are equipped for growth in your faith, strengthened and enabled by fully depending on the power of the Holy Spirit at work in your life, no longer striving to live for Christ in your own strength.

This approach instills within you the daily reminder that even in the midst of the incredible joy of the Christian life, there will be moments when sin and temptation threaten to deceive and entice you. At those times, however, when you recognize sin for what it is, you will also sense the power of the Holy Spirit working within you. It may well be that still, small, persistent voice—never strident, not discordant—quietly convicting you that one of the main tasks of the Holy Spirit is to declutter your life, to remove the temptation to sin, to set spiritual priorities for today, to enable you to recalibrate your deepest affections and to remove the regrets of the past. Now you can live with the consistent reassurance that the indwelling power of the Holy Spirit equips and enables you to know the reality of the relationship which lies behind the incredulity of David's words, 'Where can I go from your Spirit? Where can I flee from your presence? If I go up to the heavens, you are there; if I make my bed in the depths, you are there. If I rise on the wings of the dawn, if I settle on the far side of the sea, even there your hand will guide me, your right hand will hold me fast' (Ps. 139:7-10).

Questions

1) If you were to begin decluttering your life today, what areas would need immediate attention? Suggest at least three realms and explain why.

2) If 'mildly addicted to an image-rich, digitally hungry playground where meaning and purpose are determined by how connected we are to the ubiquitous convenience of the Internet' describes you, explain why.

3) David writes, 'Where can I go from your Spirit? Where can I flee from your presence?' Describe the importance of the presence of the Holy Spirit as you seek to grow and mature in your faith each day. You may wish to categorize this in the areas of worship, work, recreation, sharing the gospel, and family and friendship.

4) In discussing Luke 5:1-11, I describe Peter as meeting with God in an unexpected place. Have you ever been surprised at the places where you have encountered God? If so, explain what happened and what you learned.

5) In Romans 8, Paul writes about nurturing life in the Spirit. Explain what is involved in such a life. Are there principles from this passage that you need to apply to the messiness of your own life?

5

LIGHT IN THE DARKNESS

If I say, 'Surely the darkness will hide me
and the light become night around me,'
even the darkness will not be dark to you;
the night will shine like the day,
for darkness is as light to you.
(Ps. 139:11–12)

Questions, Questions, Questions?

Late on a Friday afternoon some years ago, I was taking my
son Michael to a dental appointment. No parking places were
available at the dentist's office, so I dropped Michael off and
parked at a nearby shopping mall. I hurried through the mall,
quickly made my way toward the dentist's office on the next
street, and jogged up four flights of stairs to access the street
adjacent to his office. As I approached his office, I suffered a
massive heart attack and almost died. I have no memory of the
days leading up to the heart attack and not much memory of the
days following it.

During the weeks immediately after the attack, I had many
questions, mainly about the details of what had taken place. It
seems that when I was approaching the dentist's office, one of his

assistants was taking out the trash after a busy day and saw me collapse on the street. As I fell, my head hit the ground, bounced up and struck it a second time. Two passersby, realizing that something was seriously wrong, put me in the recovery position, and the dentist's assistant ran back into the office, telephoned the emergency services, and explained to the dentist what had taken place. The dentist tried mouth-to-mouth resuscitation. When that failed, he used an oxygen mask to get air into my lungs in the hope that the oxygen would help sustain any brain function and vital organs. The emergency services arrived some eight to ten minutes later. They immediately checked for breathing and a pulse. Finding neither, they cut off my jacket, sweater, and shirt, and used a defibrillator to bring me back. Their fourth attempt was successful. After I was stabilized and taken to the emergency room in a nearby hospital, I suffered a second attack and was placed on a ventilator and was put into a medically induced coma. I was taken off the ventilator on Sunday morning, and eventually regained consciousness.

In the period following the heart attack, I asked numerous questions. I pestered Ruth and Michael about the details until I was able to settle in my mind what had taken place. Aside from the medical and physical questions, during the subsequent three-month recuperation period when I had plenty of time to think, the big question in my mind was this: *What was God doing in the midst of all that had taken place?*

Have you ever asked deep, probing questions about why God allowed you to go through a particularly difficult experience? Or why He seemed to be leading in a certain direction, only to steer you in another direction entirely? If so, this chapter may be just for you.

Wrestling with the Unimaginable

When David writes, 'If I say "Surely the darkness will hide me and the light become night around me," even the darkness will not be dark to you; the night will shine like the day, for darkness is as light to you' (Ps. 139:11-12), he is reminding us that, regardless of how dark the circumstances of our lives may be, despite the uncertainty we may be facing, our future is not opaque to God. In fact, God may well be the One who is behind the uncertainty.

As you continue to explore and learn from Psalm 139:11-12, I hope you will be drawn further and further into understanding the character and nature of God, and understand why, at times, it feels as if He is conspiring against all you had hoped for. Although in earlier chapters we have been mainly exploring the life of David, in this chapter—as we did in the last chapter—we will look at another individual whose life reflects the principles found in Psalm 139.

When we think of the Old Testament book of Genesis, we tend to think of Adam and Eve, Abraham and Sarah, Isaac and Rebekah, Jacob and Esau; yet fourteen chapters of Genesis focus on Joseph. More chapters are dedicated to the life of Joseph than any other character in Genesis; he has much to teach us.

In the early years of his life, Joseph does not show great promise. Like David, he comes from a modest background. A shepherd boy, he was the eleventh of twelve sons, something of a dreamer, favored by his father, and consequently disliked by his brothers. In his early years, Joseph is a seemingly insignificant individual. Yet as you look at the life of Joseph you may well ask the question, 'What was it that God saw in Joseph that brought him from being a slave when he first arrived in Egypt to being one of the most powerful leaders in the country, a close confidant of Pharaoh, a man of incorruptible character and godliness?'

When we initially meet Joseph in Genesis 37, he is seventeen years old, on the verge of early adulthood. He is probably wrestling with his identity, looking for acceptance among his family and peers, beginning to recognize his own gifts and abilities, and asking big questions about his future.

Genesis tells us that he is his father's favorite son, the child of Jacob's old age; the natural affection of a father for a son is clear. When Joseph was a little boy, I imagine that Jacob delighted to be around Joseph, constantly interacting with him, watching him grow, talking to him, playing with him, lifting him onto his knee, telling him family stories about his grandfather Isaac, and his famous great-grandfather, Abraham. Jacob would also be sure to tell Joseph about the amazing and spectacular moments when God was miraculously at work in their lives.

Jacob's affection and favoritism for Joseph were clear for all to see, especially when he gave him 'a richly ornamented robe' (Gen. 37:3). Jacob was unambiguously saying, 'Joseph, you are my favorite. You're different. You're special.' Jacob's obvious affection and special treatment of Joseph resulted in the other brothers disliking Joseph intensely. 'They hated him and could not speak a kind word to him' (Gen. 37:4). Living in a hostile, dysfunctional family environment where anger, jealousy, resentment, and hatred occur daily creates a tense and volatile atmosphere. Joseph, it seems, was oblivious to all that was taking place, and with considerable insensitivity to his brothers, he flaunted not only his coat of many colors, but his father's favoritism as well. Things were, however, about to change.

As we move further into the Genesis narrative about Joseph, we need to be careful. We are naturally tempted to think that the focal point of the unfolding story is Joseph and his brothers. Yet it is good to bear in mind that the main character of the story is not Joseph, his brothers or even their father; neither is it Joseph's famous relatives, Jacob, Isaac or even Abraham. The main character throughout Genesis, and especially in the Joseph story, is God. Whenever you find yourself engaging with a passage of Scripture, it is always worth asking what God is doing amidst a developing narrative. Why is He orchestrating and engineering the circumstances of a person's life? Discerning God at work is not always an easy task, but it is always a richly rewarding one, especially in the life of Joseph.

In Genesis 37:5, we read that 'Joseph had a dream,' and we are introduced in the most innocuous terms to a series of events that would bring dramatic and catastrophic change to Joseph, his brothers, and his father. Silently, unobtrusively, God was bringing to pass His purpose and will, yet Joseph and his family were oblivious to what God was doing. God was about to begin a refining, transforming process that would remove the privileged favoritism and domestic comforts Joseph had enjoyed.

For Joseph, God used a dream. For you, God may be working in and through the circumstances and decisions you are facing, or perhaps a situation that threatens to overwhelm you. God will use whatever it takes to bring you to a place of utter dependency on Him. When you reach that point, however, don't be surprised if God is about to do something extra special.

What is God doing?

In the early moments of God's interaction with Joseph, it is clear that He has given him the ability to interpret dreams. Joseph's first dream involves his brothers working together in a field gathering sheaves of grain. His brothers' sheaves bow down to Joseph's sheaves. A second dream reveals the sun and moon and stars bowing down to Joseph. With unrestrained excitement, he unwisely shares these dreams with his family, garnering intense hatred from his brothers. Joseph is obviously telling his brothers what the future holds, that they will bow down to him, that he will rule over them. It is clear that this young man has a remarkable gift from God. Joseph's gift is in good shape, but he—Joseph—is not.

Joseph needs significant preparation and polishing if he is ever to be the man God wants him to be. Oblivious and insensitive to what is going on in the lives of those around him, he is so enamored with his gift that he imagines his brothers will excitedly rejoice with him. Neither does Joseph anticipate that his dreams will offend his father. After all, his father loves him more than any of his brothers. Knowing his father delights in him, he expects Jacob to be pleased, perhaps to say, 'Well done, Joseph. I am so proud of you.' His father, however, is unimpressed. Clearly things are beginning to change. God has initiated the emancipation process that ultimately will lead to Joseph's being cut off from his father and brothers and everything familiar, but will also move him to a place of profound dependency on God and God alone.

At seventeen years of age, Joseph has been called and chosen by God, given an incredible gift that will enable him to become the governor of Egypt, and play a formative part in preserving the purposes and plans of God for an entire nation. But, sadly, Joseph lacks the maturity to use wisely the gift God has given him. He is so wrapped up in himself that he believes the gift is all about him and little to do with the purposes of God. At this point, Joseph knows nothing of the reality of David's affirming words, 'You hem me in—behind and before; you have laid your hand upon me. Such knowledge is too wonderful for me, too lofty for me to attain.'

There is a note of hope, however, at the end of this introductory passage on Joseph's life. 'His brothers were jealous of him, but his father kept the matter in mind' (Gen. 37:11). Why does the writer of Genesis complete this section by focusing on Jacob? Could it be that Jacob was remembering what had happened in his own life when he was not much older than Joseph? Could it be that Jacob was remembering that he had deceived his father, stolen his brother's birthright, and, on his first night away from his family's home, had also had a dream? That dream was so overwhelming and so profound that the next morning he woke up and said, 'Surely the LORD was in this place and I was not aware of it' (Gen. 28:10-19). Could it be that Jacob was remembering the transforming power of God to captivate and sustain the heart? Was the past a powerful reminder of God's ability to speak directly to Jacob's soul and draw him into a relationship of incredible intimacy? Jacob could not forget how God had worked in the past. Jacob knew from personal experience how God had worked in his own life and he kept this in mind. Could it be that Jacob was remembering that God often works in the most surprising ways?

One of the reassuring principles for us in this introduction to Joseph is the healthy reminder that we do not have to be perfect before God can begin to mold and fashion and use us for His own purposes. Joseph, and ultimately his entire family, was at the center of the plans of God, but he was not ready for what God was about to do. Joseph needed considerable refining. His relationship with God and his understanding of God needed a great deal of work. His appreciation of what he was being prepared for was nonexistent, yet God had His hand upon Joseph.

You may be feeling that in your own life you have had a bad start: parents who did not love you as they should have; limited opportunities for education growing up; struggling with a lack of self-esteem or self-confidence. You have been hurt or disappointed so badly that you still struggle with emotional wounds. The dreams you had at seventeen have not materialized the way you wished. Yet, as we have discovered, Joseph's upbringing in a dysfunctional family was not a barrier for what God was about to do.

The New Testament book of Acts highlights for us the significant difficulties Joseph faced, yet despite this we read, 'But God was with him' (Acts 7:9). This is a powerful reminder that if God is with you, no impediment, no personality difficulty, no family difficulty or lack of education or career opportunities can stand in the way of God's refining and shaping you into the person He is calling you to be. When you are facing difficult challenges, the first question you need to ask is this: *What is God doing in and through all that I am facing?*

Preparing for the Unexpected

Each Wednesday I teach a midweek Bible study class. On one occasion, much to the delight of the natural history aficionados in the group, I shared with them an article written by a delegation from the Smithsonian Natural History Museum, who had recently returned from Egypt's Nile Delta. After extensive analysis centering on the area between Alexandria in the west and Port Said in the east, the research team was able to definitively comment on the difference between the Alligator (*Alligator mississippiensis*) and the Nile Crocodile (*Crocodylus niloticus*). In addition to consideration of the overall head shape, skin color, bite pattern, and length and breadth of the snout, apparently the major difference between the alligator and crocodile is that one of them will see you later and the other will see you in a while.

As you can guess, my brief sojourn into the world of fanciful humor was not met with the reception I was hoping for. Yet it contained for me a moment of temporary contentment as my listeners believed themselves to be going in one direction and ended up discovering that they were going in an entirely different direction!

As we explore the principles behind the phrase 'even the darkness will not be dark to you' (Ps. 139:12), we find Joseph believing he is heading in a particular direction only to discover he is heading in an entirely different one, about to enter a period so dark that he probably thought life as he had known it was over.

The ever-increasing dislike of Joseph's brothers manifests itself in hatred and violence as they plan to attack and kill him. It is difficult to imagine what might be going through Joseph's mind when his older brothers turn violent, beat him, strip him of his clothes, and plan to take his life. Yet amidst the chaos of a personal and physical attack, God has other plans. Joseph's life is spared when he is sold as a slave and taken into Egypt (Gen. 37:12-36).

Exposed to a number of extraordinary challenges, Joseph comes through in a remarkable manner. As a slave, he is forced to adapt to a whole series of circumstances not of his choosing. The impact of such cataclysmic change could easily have crushed him. Yet God is continuing to prepare him in a way that he could never have imagined. The monumental upheaval Joseph encounters is sudden, with no warning, and no indication of what is to come. We can be reasonably sure, however, that he does not relish what had taken place, and as he journeys toward Egypt, we can imagine Joseph wrestling with the reality of his new circumstances and beginning to wonder if there will ever be a way back.

You may have started the kind of life that isn't what you wanted. You had little choice; your circumstances were forced upon you. It may be the result of an illness or losing your job or relocating because of your work. Perhaps you are in a marriage where there is ongoing tension and you do not know how to resolve it. Maybe you feel a little like Joseph, having experienced betrayal by a family member or a close friend. One thing is certain, however: you feel that nothing will ever be the same again. Yet when God calls and then begins to refine a person, He does it in a thorough, all-pervasive, radical manner. He never leaves anything to chance. The amazing thing, of course, is that we often do not realize what is going on while it is happening.

Life in Egypt

In Egypt, Joseph is sold as a slave into the household of Potiphar, the captain of Pharaoh's guard. In those early days, adjusting to his new circumstances, Joseph surely wished he was back home. Perhaps at night he would dream about his family, trying to remember the details of what his previous life had been, wondering if his father knew if he was alive or dead, speculating about what his brothers had said when they got back home. Joseph undoubtedly asked the more probing question, 'Why would my brothers do this to me?'

Readers of Genesis, however, know what Joseph did not know: God was actively at work. God had begun the emancipation process in the life of Joseph, though he, Joseph, was unaware of it. Away from the influence of his father and his brothers, he finds that God has removed from him everyone and everything he could depend on. Is it inconceivable that

Joseph, unaware of all that God is doing, may have wondered if God was conspiring against him? Did Joseph remember the biblical stories of his grandfather and great-grandfather, and God's faithfulness to them? I suspect that Joseph asked the same question so many others have asked down the centuries: 'If God really loves me, why would He do such a thing?' Joseph may well have felt abandoned.

In Genesis 39:1-7, we discover that, despite all that Joseph has experienced, he is doing remarkably well. We do not know how long he took to settle into his new environment in Egypt, but it is clear that he is prospering. He now lives in his master Potiphar's home as his personal assistant, and Potiphar has placed everything he owns under Joseph's care. Joseph has certainly come a long way from being a foreign slave to becoming a trusted, responsible manager, who displays outstanding competence, character, and leadership.

Even at a casual glance, the first seven verses of Genesis 39 emphasize that 'The LORD was with Joseph' (Gen. 39:2, 3, 5). The reality of the presence of God with Joseph has a significant impact on Potiphar as Joseph achieves success in all that he is involved in. It is difficult to say what is going in Potiphar's mind as he observes and interacts with Joseph, but we do know that Potiphar now trusts Joseph implicitly. It is also clear that Joseph is growing and maturing in his relationship with God as the hand of God is blessing, equipping and enabling him to succeed in his new position.

Interestingly, Joseph's immersion into his new environment and his growth and maturity seem to have nothing to do with his ability to interpret dreams. As Potiphar's personal assistant, Joseph has had no obvious opportunity to develop or use the gift that God had given him. Could it be that God was more interested in developing and maturing Joseph as a person rather than developing his gift?

God was clearly at work in Joseph's life, shaping and preparing him by teaching him lessons in leadership, integrity, and accountability. Could it be that God was impressing upon him lessons which spoke to the need for being a responsible, trustworthy man of integrity and character? Joseph, I imagine, had his own quarters and access to confidential information and household funds, as well as enjoying the complete trust of his employer. The Lord was certainly with Joseph. But just when it seemed that he was adapting and prospering in his new life, a new trial was about to come his way—a trial from an entirely unexpected source.

Surviving Temptation

The unexpected nature of a new trial for Joseph begins when we read, 'Joseph was well built and handsome' (Gen. 39:6). Potiphar's wife is attracted to Joseph and tempts him to sleep with her. Many others would have been caught off guard, flattered by the attention, but not Joseph; not even for a moment. Without hesitation, absolutely secure in himself and in his relationship with God, Joseph responds with equal boldness. We are told in simple, straightforward language – that 'he refused' (v. 8).

It is now clear that Joseph has come a long way since his days of seeking to tell his brothers and his father how much more important he was than they were. Joseph is no longer wrapped up in himself, seeking to put the focus on himself, and believing he is the most important person in any situation.

In reading these chapters, we tend to view Joseph as an extraordinary individual surrounded by some kind of supernatural protection. His response, however, tells us that it is his relationship with God that had birthed within him a commitment to live for God every day. For Joseph, the matter of sexual purity has already been settled. There is no debate in his mind; the decision does not need to be made. It had been made some time ago and he is determined not to give in to the temptation he faces. Please grasp the significance of what Joseph says: 'How could I do this great evil, and sin against God?' Joseph's relationship with God gives him the strength he needs. Remember that this is not simply a moment of weakness for Potiphar's wife; she has taunted and tempted Joseph daily over a protracted period. But from Joseph's perspective, his life is an open book before God, and by now his relationship with God is more real to him than anything or anyone else. Joseph recognizes the temptation of sin for what it is and resolutely walks away.

From Joseph's response to Potiphar's wife, it is clear that he knows the reality of the alluring, tranquilizing nature of sin, yet he refuses to surrender to it. When Potiphar's wife entices him, he flees. He does not try to negotiate with her. He does not try to reason with her. He knows he is in immediate danger. Joseph understands that when we surrender to the attraction and enticement of sin, we will ultimately find ourselves in bondage and captivity to it. The deceptive, enticing, enslaving, addictive nature of sin—a subject we explored in an earlier chapter—is a living reality to Joseph, and he refuses to surrender to its power.

When Potiphar's wife finally realizes that Joseph will not give in, her anger boils over and she concocts a story, complaining to the other servants that Joseph has approached her and tried to sleep with her. Ultimately, she complains to Potiphar, who, in turn, sends Joseph to prison, forcing Joseph to once again face a new set of circumstances not of his choosing.

When you come up against a challenging situation and someone asks you how you reacted, you may feel a sense of achievement if you have done well. But if you are tested over a prolonged period, pass the test in an exemplary fashion, and no one knows, no one encourages you, no one sends warm emails

CONSPIRACY THEORY

or texts to say, 'Well done,' no one recognizes your commitment and perseverance and achievement—that is a tough situation to find yourself in.

Difficult as it was for Joseph to have no one to encourage him, it must have been more difficult to then be punished for something he had not done. Despite being innocent, he was being treated as guilty. Joseph was being tested once again, and tested in an aggressive manner.

I suspect you have heard the saying, 'God often opens doors of opportunity on very small hinges.' But for Joseph the door being opened leads to a prison cell. Joseph has been outstanding in his response to an overwhelming temptation, but it now seems as if his faithfulness has resulted in punishment and prison. If the Lord has been with Joseph, blessing and prospering him, where was God when Joseph needed Him the most? How could God possibly allow this to happen? It certainly seems as if God was conspiring against Joseph.

If you are undergoing a trial you have never experienced before, please consider the jarring possibility that God may be paying you His highest compliment. We often seem to face the same old trials because God in His kindness allows us another opportunity to conquer them by working through them and trusting Him in the middle of them. Trials sometimes come our way in order to refine us and remove from us anything that comes between us and our relationship with God. God's single focus in allowing difficulties into our lives is to make us more Christlike. If He brings a new kind of trial into your life, it means He has definite plans for you and He is testing you to see if you can be faithful amidst the trial.

When God allows a new kind of trial, remember that He notices everything about your response—every thought and every instinctive reaction. Trials are never without significance. No matter how senseless the trial may seem, God is watching.

For Joseph, it was his relationship with God and his deep love and affection for God that kept him from falling into sin. Yet God was not finished with Joseph.

God was patiently and faithfully working in the life of Joseph. He was looking beyond the immediacy of the moment. With an eye on the future, God was focused on the deep and hidden recesses of Joseph's life, for He was preparing Joseph for greatness. While Joseph languished in prison, it seemed from his own perspective that God was silent and had allowed an innocent man to be punished. Looking on from the outside, the story of Joseph is deeply distressing. Yet the end of the chapter brings a measure of hope (Gen. 39:20-23).

Potiphar, as we know, has Joseph put in prison, the prison 'where the king's prisoners were confined' (Gen. 39:20). When a biblical author includes what at first glance seems to be unnecessary information, it is always worth paying attention; often the extraneous information is packed with significance which is only revealed as the story develops.

It is also worth recognizing in the closing verses of the chapter language similar to that of the opening verses: 'The LORD was with him; he showed him kindness and granted him favor in the eyes of the prison warden' (Gen. 39:21). This resulted in Joseph being treated well by the prison warden and 'the LORD was with Joseph and gave him success in whatever he did' (Gen. 39:23).

It is clear by the end of the chapter that, despite all that Joseph has experienced in being falsely accused and wrongly imprisoned, God has been quietly at work bringing to pass His purpose and His will. Here we see the principles of Psalm 139:11-12 playing a part in all that Joseph was experiencing. 'Surely the darkness will hide me and the light become night around me, even the darkness will not be dark to you; the night will shine like the day, for darkness is as light to you'

(Ps. 139:11-12). Despite the darkness and despair of prison life, God was far from finished with Joseph.

The Why of Waiting

Today, we live in a world of instant gratification. If you need an answer to a sports question or have an insatiable desire to know the population of Kathmandu or wonder who won the Nobel Prize for Economics in 1994 or an Oscar in 2002, you can simply Google it. If you do not like a television program you are watching, you can try Netflix, Amazon Prime, Hulu, or check for digital movies you can access on your phone or tablet. If you are standing in a supermarket line waiting to check out, you may find yourself tempted to examine the line next to you and sigh if your line is not moving quickly enough. No one likes waiting in traffic, or waiting for food to be served—and of course you are checking emails, Facebook, and texting while you are waiting. Yet, there are moments in your life worth waiting for—moments you know you should not rush through—moments that you need to savor, appreciate, and enjoy. Striving toward graduation, investing in a marriage, raising children, and persevering in a tough working environment while you learn and grow your career. Waiting can be rewarding, but it often does not feel that way when you are in the midst of it and see no reason for it.

As Genesis 39 ends, Joseph has been wrongly accused and incarcerated; yet 'the LORD was with him.' Genesis 40 begins, 'Some time later, the cupbearer and the baker of the king of Egypt offended their master, the king of Egypt.' Strangely enough, they were imprisoned under the watchful eye of Joseph. Coincidence? Happenstance? Providence?

If you carefully read chapter 40, you begin to see a connection that is not immediately obvious. There is just a hint of something else taking place when twice within a few verses you read, 'some time later' and 'after they had been in prison some time.' Within the passage there is a clear emphasis on the *timing* of the events taking place.

One of the things you may find hardest in the Christian life is being totally content with God's timing. If you are living according to your own schedule and your own timetable, you may be tempted to believe that you know best. After all, you know what needs to be done. No one knows the situation better than you do, and you have better understanding and greater insight into what is happening than anyone else and you can, therefore, find the perfect solution to resolve it.

Being confident in and utterly dependent on God and His timing is not easy. It is difficult to trust God when you're trying to make Him conform to your timing.

It was this principle that Joseph had to learn. This principle needed to become part of who he was, part of his identity. God selected Joseph as a chief instrument in His redemptive plan, a plan and a purpose that would live for generations—a plan that would impact a nation and have a ripple effect that reverberated throughout the history of Israel. But Joseph had to wait for his time to come because he had to wait upon God's perfect timing.

Joseph was a man in preparation; God had been preparing him all of his life. Like most of us, you couldn't have told Joseph that he needed more preparation. You may believe you are ready just as you are. Yet God used the darker side of providence to prepare Joseph even further.

The doctrine of the providence of God is not an easy concept to grasp, especially when we are going through a difficult and painful experience. Understanding what is meant by 'providence' definitely helps:

> God, the great Creator of all things, does uphold, direct, dispose, and govern all creatures, actions, and things from the greatest even to the least, by His most wise and holy providence, according to His infallible foreknowledge, and the free and immutable counsel of His own will, to the praise of the glory of His wisdom, power, justice, goodness, and mercy.[1]

If you're going to find light in the midst of darkness, there are truths in Genesis 40–41 that you must grasp, be committed to, and apply to your life. Providence reminds us that, during the darkest of times, during days of disappointment and distrust, God is still at work and you can trust Him despite the pain you are experiencing.

It is an incredibly painful moment when a sick five-year-old is taken to the doctor and is diagnosed as having an allergic reaction and needing an injection in order to survive. When the child sees the doctor approaching with a needle, he naturally runs to his dad for protection. Yet the same dad who has in the past kissed scrapes and provided hugs of comfort now holds down his five-year-old while the doctor administers the painful remedy. At age five, you cannot comprehend that what you need most is the thing that will cause so much pain.

A maturing and growing faith is at times a painful process. Joseph is about to learn that if his joy is rooted in his own comfort, his joy cannot last. But if his joy is rooted in the character of God, it will never desert him. The dark side of providence drives you into the arms of a Father who lives above the here and now and the emotion of the moment. 'Even the darkness will not be dark to you; the night will shine like the day, for darkness is as light to you' (Ps. 139:11-12).

---

1. Westminster Confession of Faith (Chapter 5:1).

Vindication Finally?

As Genesis 40 continues, the focus shifts in an unexpected manner from Joseph to the cupbearer and the baker. Both the cupbearer and the baker had angered Pharaoh, and, in the providence of God, they are now in prison under Joseph's supervision. Each of them has a dream. The dreams contain imagery and symbolism difficult to understand, but we know what the cupbearer and the baker do not know: Joseph can interpret dreams. At long last it looks as though Joseph will be able to use the gift that God had given him all those years ago.

When Joseph realizes what is taking place, he asks what their dreams were about. When they explain, Joseph's response seems so natural: 'Do not interpretations belong to God?' He does not say this to sound impressive or knowledgeable. Joseph, despite—or because of—all that he has gone through, is now at the point in his maturing relationship with God where he instinctively displays a principle we explored in earlier chapters. He does the natural things spiritually and the spiritual things naturally.

Joseph listens to the dreams and interprets them, and over the next few days his interpretations come true. The cupbearer lives but the chief baker dies. Now Joseph sees in this new development an opportunity to gain his freedom. I imagine Joseph thinking to himself, 'Surely God has brought this to pass. Finally God is at work. He has heard my prayers and I will be free. LORD, thank You. Please forgive me for the moments when I doubted You. I should have trusted more in Your providential care. I will be free at last.'

In a brief conversation packed with possibilities, Joseph turns to the cupbearer and tells him how he had been forcibly removed from his homeland, sold into slavery, and wrongly imprisoned. Then he adds, 'When all goes well with you, remember me and show me kindness; mention me to Pharaoh and get me out of this prison' (Gen. 40:14). His plea to the cupbearer is 'remember me.' Sadly, the chapter ends disappointingly for him. 'The chief cupbearer, however, did not remember Joseph; he forgot him' (Gen. 40:23).

The unanswered question at the end of the chapter is, *Why would the cupbearer forget Joseph?* Surely God was at work. Why would God act like this? Could He not have nudged the cupbearer a little and reminded him of Joseph?

In those early moments of the cupbearer's release, Joseph may well have been thinking that, since the cupbearer was only in prison for three days, and since he has now been restored to a position of power and influence, things could change any moment. But one day creeps past, and then another. Days turn into weeks, and weeks into months. It is easy to imagine Joseph distraught and in despair, weeping with frustration and disappointment—the disappointment of unanswered prayers. What was God doing? What was to be served by keeping Joseph in prison?

Consider all that had taken place during Joseph's painful time in prison. What was God now teaching Joseph? Why would He allow Joseph to remain in prison? Could it be that Joseph was in need of further preparation? Could it be that he still had lessons to learn? Was Joseph attempting to nudge the hand of providence when he asked the cupbearer to remember him when he was returned to a position of influence? Was this evidence that Joseph needed further preparation and further maturing? When Joseph felt he needed to push himself forward, pull some strings, get his name out there, advance himself a little, God, as it were, shook His head and said, 'Joseph, don't you trust Me? Let Me handle this. You really can depend on Me. You can trust Me. I can do this.' Joseph still had to learn one of the hardest lessons to learn in the Christian life. When you are willing to stop interfering, when you come to an end of yourself, with nowhere else to go and nothing else to say, and utterly and entirely surrender and submit every area of your life to the rule and reign of God, then—and only then—are you ready to move forward.

Many years ago, J. I. Packer wrote a classic book called *Knowing God* which sold millions of copies. In one particularly striking section, he writes about the darker side of providence:

> He blesses those on whom he sets his love in a way that humbles them, so that all the glory may be his alone. He hates the sins of his people, and uses all kinds of inward and outward pains and griefs to wean their hearts from compromise and disobedience. He seeks the fellowship of his people, and sends them both sorrows and joys in order to detach their love from other things and attach it to himself. He teaches believers to value his promised gifts by making them wait for those gifts, and compelling them to pray persistently for them, before he bestows them. So we read of God dealing with his people in the Scripture record, and so he deals with them still. His aims and principles of action remain consistent; he does not at any time act out of character. Our ways, we know, are pathetically inconstant—but not God's.[2]

Over the next two years, God continued to work in the life of Joseph.

If you have ever been frustrated at the timing of His providence, and you have prayed, and waited, and longed for God to work in a particular way, you will know that a period of two years feels like an eternity. It can seem as though God has forgotten you and is conspiring against you.

There may be times in your life when you cannot possibly comprehend why God allows problems into your life that cause

---

2. J. I. Packer, *Knowing God* (London, England: Hodder & Stoughton, 1988), p. 88.

you pain and grief and disappointment, but in the process He may take you to a place where you learn to entirely cast yourself on Him—a place where you come to the end of your own strength so that you no longer rely on yourself. At the beginning of this chapter I asked, 'What was it that God saw in Joseph that brought him from being a slave when he first arrived in Egypt, to being one of the most powerful leaders in the country, a close confidant of Pharaoh, a man of incorruptible character and godliness?' Now we can answer the question. It was not so much what God saw in Joseph, but what Joseph saw in God and experienced under His refining hand that enabled him to ultimately, utterly, and profoundly depend on the Lord alone.

Many years ago, the movie actor Jimmy Stewart lost a son in the Vietnam War. Despite the terrible pain involved, he was eventually able to get to the place where he understood the reality of the truths contained within a poem he received at that time.

> 'In pastures green'? No, not always so, sometimes He
> Who knoweth best in kindness leadeth me
> In weary ways, where heavy shadows be;
> Out of the sunshine, warm, and soft, and bright,
> Out of the sunshine into darkest night.
> I oft would faint with sorrow and of fright.
> Only for this: I know He holds my hand;
> So, whether in a green or desert land,
> I trust Him, though I do not always understand.
>
> And 'by still waters'? No, not always so.
> Oft times the heavy tempests round me blow,
> And o'er my soul the waves and billows go.
> But when the storm beats loudest, and I cry
> Aloud for help, the Master standeth by,
> And whispers to my soul, 'Lo, it is I.'

Above the tempest wild I hear Him say,
'Beyond this darkness lies the perfect day;
In every path of thine I lead the way.'

So whether on the hilltops high and fair
I dwell, or in the sunless valleys where
The shadows lie—what matters? He is there.
And more than this, where'er the pathway lead
He gives to me no helpless broken reed,
But His own hand, sufficient for my need.
So where ere He leads me I can safely go;
And in the blest hereafter I shall know
Why, in His wisdom, He hath led me so.

It is not so much what God sees in you, but what you see in
God and experience under His loving, refining hand that
enables you to ultimately to depend on Him and prayerfully
say, 'Surely the darkness will hide me and the light become
night around me, even the darkness will not be dark to you;
the night will shine like the day, for darkness is as light to you'
(Ps. 139:11-12).

Questions

1) When God was initially at work in the life of Joseph, he was seventeen years old. Were you aware of God interacting with you at age seventeen? Describe your relationship with Him and all that you hoped your future would hold for you when you were a teenager.

2) Joseph's brothers disliked him immensely and eventually sold him into slavery. What was your relationship like with your siblings when you were growing up? What role did your family play in making you the person you are?

3) Joseph began to grow in his faith, and we read that, while he was in Potiphar's house, 'the LORD was with [him].' Explain how an individual matures in his or her faith, and specify what is involved. You may wish to expand your answer to consider areas such as (a) developing a godly character, (b) overcoming temptation, and (c) managing in situations where your prayers do not seem to be heard and answered.

4) Explain the significance of God's providence and why it is wonderfully reassuring. List at least two specific examples from either your experience or from your general knowledge.

5) Explain why it is so difficult sometimes to trust in God's timing. What principles have you learned in this chapter that might encourage you, and others, to be more at peace in the matter of His timing?

6

CREATED FOR A PURPOSE

For you created my inmost being;
you knit me together in my mother's womb.
I praise you because I am fearfully and wonderfully made;
your works are wonderful, I know that full well.
My frame was not hidden from you when I was
made in the secret place. When I was woven together
in the depths of the earth, your eyes saw my unformed body.
All the days ordained for me were written in your book
before one of them came to be.
(Ps. 139:13–16)

'But God...'

A friend recently sent me an email that caused me to laugh out loud. I enjoy humor as much as the next person, but I rarely laugh out loud. The reason for my audible outburst was the question contained in the email: 'Have you ever woken up glad to be alive and given the person next to you a big kiss? I did earlier today, and I will not be allowed to fly with that airline again.'

It is relatively easy to sense that the focus of Psalm 139:13-14 stimulates and strengthens a 'glad to be alive' feeling when you recognize the reality contained within David's words: 'For you created my inmost being; you knit me together in my mother's womb. I praise you because I am fearfully and wonderfully made; your works are wonderful, I know that full well.' Yet despite David's reassuring words, we often find our thinking dominated by the circumstances around us rather than by the enabling promises of God.

In the previous chapter, we focused on the challenges Joseph faced and sought to empathize with him. His life had been marred by an indulgent father, dysfunctional brothers, personal rejection, deep disappointment, slavery, and false accusations. Toward the end of Genesis 40, a note of hope creeps into the story when Joseph meets Pharaoh's chief cupbearer. Then those hopes are dashed when we read, 'The chief cupbearer, however, did not remember Joseph; he forgot him.' I don't imagine that Joseph would be waking up full of energy and filled with optimism as time creeps past and he begins to realize he will not be freed from prison any time soon. It is worth remembering that although others had forgotten Joseph, God had not.

When David writes, 'You created my inmost being; you knit me together in my mother's womb. I praise you because I am fearfully and wonderfully made; your works are wonderful, I know that full well' (Ps. 139:13-14), he is writing from a position of realizing the enormity of God's overwhelming love lavished upon him. Yet for Joseph it would be another two years before he would find himself appreciating at a new level the extravagant love of God.

During those two years Joseph would rediscover the reality of a biblical principle God had previously taught him: *If his joy is rooted in his own comfort, then his joy could not last. But if his joy is rooted in the character and nature of God, then his joy would not desert him.*

Joseph was learning the hard way, being prepared for what was still to come. His character, nature, and profound dependence on the living God were being forged by patience and longsuffering. He now had to wrestle with God's timing, recognizing that God's delays are not always God's denials. The word 'longsuffering' sums up Joseph's experience from the beginning of his enforced exile to Egypt. It is easy to imagine that he would be tempted to give up on God and ask, 'What is the point? My entire life has been one huge disappointment after another.' He may have cried himself to sleep from sheer frustration, feeling that his heart had been broken, his life amounted to very little, and he had been abandoned.

He was about to learn, however, that the heartfelt love of God is not lavished upon us only for a season. The love that transforms the soul is not based upon a temporary or casual relationship. He was discovering that, in the most intimate of moments, the steadfast love of God never ceases; His love is persistent and unchanging as He invests in His children for the long haul.

As the prison door was closing and future opportunities were opening, Joseph was unaware of God's plan. Surely he wondered why God would delay his release from prison. God's purposes often include seemingly endless delays from our perspective, but Joseph—like millions of others—would come to learn that God's timing is perfect.

Pharaoh had a Dream...

In the dark, deceptive atmosphere of prison, Joseph was beginning to understand that pain can shape a life for greatness. History is filled with stories of those whose struggles and scars formed the foundation for remarkable achievements. Amidst hardship, they gained what they needed to achieve greatness. There are significant benefits that come only through struggles. Author A. W. Tozer once wrote, 'It is doubtful whether God can bless a man greatly until He has hurt him deeply.'[1] Joseph would undoubtedly agree.

---

1. A. W. Tozer, *The Root of the Righteous* (Camp Hill, PA: Christian Publications, 1986), p. 136.

As the Genesis narrative continues to develop, chapter 41 reveals that two long years drag by, and I imagine Joseph concludes that nothing of significance is taking place and he had been forgotten. Yet it only seemed like nothing was happening; in reality a great deal was taking place. Joseph was quietly being strengthened, refined, and perfected. Then without warning, amidst the mundane and the routine of daily life, 'Pharaoh had a dream' (Gen. 41:1). Please understand the significance of those four words. It was not the cupbearer whom Joseph had helped who had the dream. Neither was it the prison governor. It was Pharaoh, and it was not one dream, but two.

The next morning when Pharaoh called for his wise men, they were unable to help him. The moment Joseph has longed for finally arrives: the cupbearer remembers Joseph. After two years of waiting, after all of the hurt, the pain, and the disappointment, God intervenes. At last it seems as though God is bringing to pass His purposes and will, with Joseph at the center of them.

At this point in the Joseph narrative, you may find yourself thinking, 'It is about time!' Then you realize that you know more about what is taking place than Joseph does. Joseph knows nothing about the situation in Pharaoh's palace. He has no inkling of God's unfolding plans.

Imagine what is going through Joseph's mind. It has been several years since he lived a normal life. Now out of the blue Pharaoh sends for him. Amidst a flurry of activity, Joseph finds himself washed, freshly shaven, wearing a clean robe, and standing before Pharaoh. He may well have been a little nervous and on edge, yet when Pharaoh speaks to him, he is calm, collected, and completely in control. He has become a changed man, ready at last to respond to God's perfect timing.

When Pharaoh explains to Joseph his need for someone to interpret his dreams, Joseph responds with remarkable integrity and humility. 'I cannot do it,' Joseph replies, 'but God will give Pharaoh the answer he desires' (Gen. 41:16). Joseph is indeed a changed man.

In the past, Joseph may have considered this a golden opportunity to set the record straight. 'Pharaoh, I have been unjustly incarcerated for a crime I did not commit. Two years ago, I met your cupbearer and accurately interpreted a dream for him. Yet upon his own freedom he instantly forgot what I had done for him. For the past two years I could have been serving you and interpreting your dreams. Please grant me justice by removing him from your court and I will interpret your dreams.'

Joseph responds to Pharaoh, however, with remarkable maturity, refusing to draw attention to the time he has served in prison or the circumstances leading up to his imprisonment. Joseph's heart has been reshaped by the heat of affliction. The circumstances surrounding his imprisonment and his years of isolation have moved him to a place of deep dependence on the living God. The darker side of providence is, at last, revealing God's purpose and design amidst the personal pain he has experienced.

For the rest of his life, Joseph refuses to live with resentment and bitterness. He does not verbally abuse his brothers who had sold him into slavery. He bears no grudge against Potiphar's wife. Nor does he berate the cupbearer who had forgotten him. Even though he is now in a position to get even, Joseph does not do so. He is contented to leave such matters in the hands of God. Talk about maturity, character, and integrity: here is a man prepared by God for greatness. The preparation had been painful, radical, comprehensive, and prolonged; yet through it all, 'the LORD was with Joseph.'

As Pharaoh highlights the details of his dreams, Joseph responds in a clear and succinct manner. Egypt on a national scale will have seven years of abundant harvests, followed by seven years of severe famine, which will cause the people to forget the years of plenty. Joseph completes the interpretation by reminding Pharaoh that the purposes of God shall come to pass, and that Pharaoh should be prepared for what is coming. It is now clear that Joseph was created for a purpose—a purpose much greater than he could ever have dreamed of.

Joseph's Focus

As we look back over the previous chapters of the Joseph narrative, it is fascinating to see a pattern emerge. Joseph mentions God once in chapter 39, once in chapter 40, but on five occasions in chapter 41. Although the circumstances of his life dominate the earlier chapters, God is standing in the shadows with His purposes underlying all that is taking place. In chapter 41, Joseph's focus is no longer on himself, but firmly on the purposes and plans of God. He consistently refers to God in his conversation with Pharaoh. Instead of calling attention to himself, he points Pharaoh heavenward. Now recognizing he has been created for a purpose, Joseph has truly humbled himself under the mighty hand of God.

Further evidence of Joseph's personal maturity and profound dependence on God comes to the fore as the chapter develops. In response to the challenges Egypt faces as a nation, Joseph provides wise and insightful counsel for Pharaoh: 'And now let Pharaoh look for a man discerning and wise, and set him over the land of Egypt.' Along with this recommendation, Joseph advises Pharaoh to find someone with remarkable leadership skills—able to take responsibility for managing the seven years of abundant crops, oversee the building of granaries, and regulate the supply and demand process, while storing up grain for the seven years of famine.

Although challenging, the situation ahead is clear. Pharaoh will need an individual with discipline and foresight, someone in whom Pharaoh's trust would be implicit, someone who can handle the most challenging of responsibilities on a national level. At no time did Joseph suggest he was the individual most capable for the job. There was no more putting himself in the picture, no more 'Remember me!' requests. I am convinced it never even crossed his mind.

Steadfastly refusing to manipulate the moment, Joseph advises Pharaoh and then waits. Through the loneliness and isolation of prison, feeling abandoned and forgotten, Joseph had learned to let God have His way, knowing that, in His own time, God would unfold His eternal plans. Now utterly devoid of ambition, Joseph refuses to promote himself. How wonderfully refreshing, how rare—and, more importantly, how exciting—to see God's unfolding plans both for Joseph and for Egypt.

How, then, do we begin to apply this lesson to our own lives? Have you ever found yourself tempted to maneuver a situation to your own advantage, only to regret it when you have achieved it? It can be a deeply humiliating experience to manipulate circumstances to acquire what you longed for, and then see it wither away once you have attained it. That kind of elevation or promotion did not interest Joseph. At this stage in his relationship with God, he knew that if God was in it, God would do it. It had all started with the unpromising, innocuous words, 'Pharaoh had a dream.' Joseph had no desire to nudge the hand of God or manipulate a situation to his own advantage. What came next, however, was far from innocuous. God's time had come for Joseph.

Like so many new beginnings in our own lives, the next chapter for Joseph begins with a question. Pharaoh consulted his officials and asked, 'Can we find anyone like this man, one in whom is the spirit of God?' Then Pharaoh said to Joseph, 'Since God has made all of this known to you, there is no one so discerning and wise as you. You shall be in charge of my palace, and all my people are to submit to your orders. Only with respect to the throne will I be greater than you' (Gen. 41:38-40).

Now, at last Joseph, sees the purpose he has been created for—a purpose much greater than he could have initially imagined, much greater than his ability to interpret dreams; a purpose God had in mind when He created Joseph in his mother's womb; a purpose that led to a broken and contrite heart, a heart forged by affliction, bruised and wounded by disappointment and unrealized dreams. God slowly reveals to Joseph that He has not conspired against him, but has in fact walked beside him through it all.

When the years of affliction and frustration end, Joseph emerges with his character refined, his emotional life stable, and a profound dependence not on the circumstances of his life but on God Himself. By the end of chapter 41, Joseph, now thirty years old, married with two children, has achieved power, influence, and prestige. But this is not the end of the story.

Joseph has learned the reality of living each day with a theocentric focus. Although he has many more years to live, the years of preparation have enabled him to become the man God was calling him to be. This was not the beginning of the end, but it was the end of the beginning.

Imago Dei

Having explored the life of Joseph and other biblical characters, we find it remarkable how God has clearly created each one of them for a purpose. David, lost in wonder, writes, 'For you created my inmost being; you knit me together in my mother's womb. I praise you because I am fearfully and wonderfully made; your works are wonderful, I know that full well. My frame was not hidden from you when I was made in the secret place. When I was woven together in the depths of the earth, your eyes saw my unformed body.' David is not only marveling that God created him for a purpose, but is also in awe of God's creative initiative in life itself.

Although David reminds us that we do not see what transpires in the 'secret place' (the womb), today science can tell us when a heartbeat is detectible, brain waves are present, cartilage and bone are observable, and fingerprints and DNA exist. He is powerfully reminding his readers that when God formed us in the womb, it was not by chance or accident. God was intentional in His design and purpose.

In the Genesis creation account, we read that we are set apart from the rest of God's created order: 'Then God said, "Let us make man in our image, in our likeness, and let them rule over the fish of the sea and the birds of the air, over the livestock, over all the earth, and over all the creatures that move along the ground." So God created man in his own image' (Gen. 1:26-27). In the second chapter of Genesis we see more details of humanity's divine distinctiveness, as God 'breathed into his nostrils the breath of life, and the man became a living being' (Gen. 2:7).

In recognizing that we were made in the image of God and life is given by Him, we are therefore not only set apart from the rest of God's created order, but we are also endowed with the inalienable qualities of a rational, relational, reflective, free, intelligent, moral religious agent, capable by grace of growing in knowledge, righteousness, and holiness in the image of our Creator and in relationship with the rest of humanity.

Having been made in the image of God and bearing His likeness, Christians believe in the sanctity of human life. From God's creative action in conception and gestation to natural death, the Scriptures teach that life is sacred.

We have seen society's commitment to the sanctity of human life expressed in response to suicide bombers bringing violence, trauma, and carnage to public markets in Iraq; terrorist attacks at rock concerts in Paris and Manchester, England; multiple beheadings by ISIS in Libya, Syria, and elsewhere; attacks on crowds in Germany and London; and Egyptian pilgrims blown up while at worship. Such events shock, sadden, and outrage us. This type of attack—and sadly there are too many of them—are condemned across the world as the barbaric taking of innocent life.

Most of us, however, do not know the people involved in these attacks and may never visit the places involved, but our strong expression of outrage is directly related to our commitment to the belief of the priority and sanctity of human life. This concept lies at the heart of who we are, and in many ways defines what it means to be a member of the human race.

The principle of the sanctity of human life is also enshrined in the United States Declaration of Independence: 'We hold these truths to be self-evident, that all men are created equal, that they are endowed by their Creator with certain unalienable rights, that among these are Life, Liberty and the pursuit of Happiness.'[2] When we acknowledge, 'we hold these truths to be self-evident,' we mean these truths are obvious to all, not open to debate. The United Nations code highlights a similar principle in its statement, Universal Declaration of Human Rights, Article 3: 'Everyone has the right to life, liberty and security of person.'[3]

---

2.   http://www.ushistory.org/declaration/document/
3.   http://www.un.org/en/universal-declaration-human-rights/

Defining Life?

After reflecting on what it means to be made in the image of God and society's commitment to the sanctity of human life, we see David's challenge in Psalm 139:13-16 to consider the sacredness of life in the womb. As we explore these verses, it is difficult to avoid certain questions: When does an individual become a person? What is the essence of personhood? What is the role of a developing intelligence that has a self-conscious personal thought and the ability to communicate? Does making moral choices and being responsible for those choices determine whether someone is a person or not?

Christian ethicists have long argued that since human beings are made in the image of God, personhood, human value, and dignity are derived from an individual's membership in the human race. Others, however, would not agree about the details of what constitutes personhood. Issues relating to medical ethics, procreative technology, embryo experimentation, ventilatory support systems, artificial insemination, *in vitro* fertilization, euthanasia, and a women's right to choose her reproductive circumstances are all issues that society wrestles with.

If we are to be equipped, however, to live out our faith in the messiness, challenges, and distractions of daily living, we will regularly come into contact with issues that make us feel uncomfortable or uncertain about how to respond. Yet these are often the moments when we begin to grow in our faith as God challenges us about living out our Christian values amidst a difficult setting.

Imagine that you are a thirty-one-year-old mother of three children, ages five, three, and one. As you drop off your children at daycare, you bump into your best friend, Anne, a dental hygienist who has four children under eight years old. As you meet in the corridor, it is obvious something is wrong. Anne is not her usual bright self; she gives a quick smile and hurries past. When you return to your car and text her, she texts back, 'Can't talk. Will call tonight.'

That night, she begins to cry when she hears your voice. Eventually she composes herself and explains what is going on. Her husband John has been told that he will lose his job at the end of the month, and about a week ago they discovered that they are expecting a new baby. Anne confesses that she is not sure she can cope, and as a couple they are considering an abortion. What do you say? How do you respond? Anne is your best friend. You love her dearly. How should you advise her? How does your faith equip you to engage in the issue of abortion and the sanctity of human life?

There is no question that abortion is a sensitive and controversial subject that can cause passionate, highly charged discussions and often generate more heat than light. Abortion is, for many people, a complex issue with no easy answer. It is a profoundly ethical issue—at its heart an issue of life or death. The question at the epicenter of the issue asks this: 'Is the fetus in the womb a life, or is it simply an undifferentiated mass of tissue?'

Despite the complex and controversial issues surrounding the question of life in the womb, science is clear on the following:

- The Mayo Clinic reports that approximately 21 days following conception, the fetus develops a heart, which begins to pump blood approximately 28 days after conception.[4]

- The American Pregnancy Association explains that during the fourth week following conception, the lungs, jawbone, and nasal cavity begin to develop. During this period, the hands and feet develop small buds that eventually

---

4. https://www.reference.com/health/many-days-after-conception-human-fetus-begin-heartbeat-f157adc9ea29a66c#

become fingers and toes. During the fifth week following fertilization, every bodily organ has developed.[5]

- Week five is the start of the 'embryonic period.' This is when all the baby's major systems and structures develop. The embryo's cells multiply and start to take on specific functions. This is called differentiation. Blood cells, kidney cells, and nerve cells develop. The embryo grows rapidly, and the baby's external features begin to form. The baby's brain, spinal cord, and heart begin to develop, and the gastrointestinal tract starts to form.[6]

- Weeks six to seven, arm and leg buds start to grow. The baby's brain forms into five different areas. Some cranial nerves are visible. Eyes and ears begin to form. The baby's heart continues to grow and now beats at a regular rhythm. Blood pumps through the main vessels.[7]

- Week eight, arms and legs have grown longer. Hands and feet begin to form and look like little paddles. The baby's brain continues to grow, and the lungs start to form.[8]

- Week nine, nipples and hair follicles form. Arms grow and elbows develop. Baby's toes can be seen. All baby's essential organs have begun to grow.[9]

Dr. Keith L. Moore, world-renowned embryologist and author of a number of definitive embryology books for medical students, writes: 'A zygote [fertilized egg] is the beginning of a new human being. Human development begins at fertilization, the process during which a male gamete… unites with a female

5. Ibid.
6. https://medlineplus.gov/ency/article/002398.htm
7. Ibid.
8. Ibid.
9. Ibid.

gamete or oocyte... to form a single cell called a zygote. This highly specialized, totipotent cell marks the beginning of each of us as a unique individual.' [10] Seeking to be even clearer about the issue of when life begins, Moore writes: '[The zygote], formed by the union of an oocyte and a sperm, is the beginning of a new human being.'[11]

On April 23-24, 1982, a United States Senate Judiciary Subcommittee held hearings on the question of when human life begins, and sought input from the scientific community. A group of internationally recognized biologists and geneticists confirmed that human life begins at the point of conception (fertilization). The Subcommittee on Separation of Powers to Senate Judiciary Committee S-158, Report, 97th Congress, 1st Session, 1981, concluded: 'Physicians, biologists, and other scientists agree that conception marks the beginning of the life of a human being—a being that is alive and is a member of the human species. There is overwhelming agreement on this point in countless medical, biological, and scientific writings.'[12]

Finally, science tells us that the entire genetic code—which determines a person's physical characteristics (height, face shape, hair and eye color)—is established at the point of conception. Not 21 days after or 36 days after, but at the point of conception. From the very beginning, the fetus is a human child, and the child's humanity is verifiable in every cell of the body.[13]

---

10. K. L. Moore, *The Developing Human: Clinical Orientated Embryology* (7th edition, Philadelphia, PA: Saunders, 2003), p. 27.

11. Keith L. Moore, *Before We Are Born: Essentials of Embryology* (7th edition, Philadelphia, PA: Saunders, 2008), p. 2.

12. Report, Subcommittee on Separation of Powers to Senate Judiciary Committee S-158, 97th Congress, 1st Session 1981, p. 7.

13. https://www.babycenter.com/2_inside-pregnancy-your-babys-dna_10354440.bc

Science is not in doubt that in the womb life exists, the genetic code is intact, brainwaves are evident, and a heartbeat exists.

Yet some would disagree and articulate what is called the 'actuality principle,' which argues that a person has the right to life only when capable of functioning in an intellectual, moral, social manner, conscious of surroundings, and capable of independent thought and reflection. Until an individual is capable of being a personal functioning entity, the person has no right to life.

When I was seriously ill I had to spend a weekend in an Intensive Care Unit on life support. During those three days, I was not capable of acting in an intellectual, moral, social manner, conscious of my surroundings and capable of independent thought and reflection. Should my family have simply concluded that my existence was not life as I had known it and switched off my life-support machine?

Consider the 'actuality' principle from another angle: Your baby boy was born moments ago, wrapped up, and laid in your arms. Is that baby capable of functioning in an intellectual, moral, social manner, conscious of his surroundings and capable of independent thought and reflection?

When we focus on the priority and sanctity of human life, we are called upon to look after the rights of the life in the womb, as well as looking after the life of the woman involved. In addition to this, we are also seeking to assist mothers who may find themselves wrestling with the possibility of abortion.

Only three percent of abortions today are for the so-called 'hard' cases of rape, incest, and preserving the life of the mother. With crisis pregnancy care, moral education, and protective legislation, babies and mothers alike can be protected. Options for healthy pregnancy and adoption are available, despite the difficult situation such moms find themselves in.

Some time ago, my congregation spent a Sunday morning exploring the issue of abortion and how to respond to this sensitive and emotionally complex issue. The message included the following letter written by a lady in the congregation.

My first abortion was at age eighteen. I was young, naïve, and one of the 'good girls.' He was handsome, a pastor's son, and a few years older. He was my first love. He gave me a pre-engagement ring and I gave him my virginity. My mother and the doctor arranged for the abortion to be in the hospital, and I was told it was just a blob of tissue. Afterwards, the abortion was never talked about by my family or my boyfriend. It was as if it never happened. It caused our relationship to end, I was heartbroken, and my innocence was shattered. Consequently, my life took an entirely different direction than it would have, had I done things God's way.

My second abortion was at age twenty-four. My boyfriend of three years insisted I have the abortion. I sobbed as he yelled at me all the way to the abortion clinic. He dropped me off, paid for it, and went to work. I had never felt so alone or full of despair as that day—I don't remember a lot about it. I only told one good friend what had happened, but not my mother. I was too ashamed. That relationship broke up shortly after the abortion as well. In 1981, at age twenty-seven, I got pregnant again. This time I knew, without a doubt, that I could not have another abortion. The father wanted to keep the baby, so we chose life and marriage. We had two more beautiful children and were married for eleven years until he died suddenly.

During my years as a single mother, God was pursuing me, and finally I surrendered and gave my life to Him. I finally accepted that He truly loved me and that I was forgiven of all the sins of my past. God redeemed me and gave me a brand-new life in Christ!

Thirty-five years after my first abortion, I attended a 'Forgiven and Set Free' Bible Study given by Piedmont Women's Center. There I learned that God had 'removed my sins as far as the east is from the west' and 'would remember them no more!' I was truly healed and set free from the guilt and shame I had carried all those years. Now my life verse is: 'Fear not, for I have redeemed you, I have called you by name—you are mine!' (Isaiah 43:1)

The difference between my old life and new life in Christ has been a miraculous testimony of God's transforming and redeeming love, grace, and mercy. Oh, and the baby daughter I chose life for got married in 2001 and has blessed me with two precious grandchildren that I love with all my heart and thank God for every day! Thank you, Lord, for eternally changing my family tree!

Abortion is not an easy subject to wrestle with, yet when we hold firmly to the sanctity of human life, we must respond with love, care, sensitivity, and compassion to those who have been wounded and continue to grieve the loss of their child. Prayerful support, counseling, and a tender approach are vital to those who are struggling, combined with the assurance that the transforming love of God can help ease the pain, heal the wounds, and restore those involved to a fresh beginning. God does not abandon us when we make poor choices, sin against Him, or find ourselves in the most difficult of circumstances. God has indeed created us for a purpose, and He is not ready to give up on us yet.

Protected for a Purpose

When David writes, 'All the days ordained for me were written in your book before one of them came to be' (Ps. 139:16), he is reminding his readers that every life is not only sacred but each of us has a purpose. That purpose may be unexpected or difficult to discover but His promise is nevertheless real.

Toward the beginning of the Old Testament book of Exodus (Exod. 2:1-10), the dramatic telling of the birth of Moses is a powerful narrative packed with tension and drama replete with twists and turns. While the dark shadow of infanticide provides a palpable sense of suspense, the quickly unfolding excitement is also a powerful reminder of the priority and sanctity of life, and that each person is created for a purpose. It is the unexpected ending of the story, however, that captures our attention. We see God bringing together two groups of people who, in Moses' day, would not willingly associate with each other.

When baby Moses first opened his eyes, no one in his family could anticipate the impact his birth would have. They never imagined that Moses would come to be defined by the phrase, 'The LORD would speak to Moses face to face, as one speaks to a friend' (Exod. 33:11). When David writes, 'For you created my inmost being; you knitted me together in my mother's womb,' these words could have been written by Moses. Moses was, in the providence of God, created for a purpose, and although he did not know it, this was clear from the earliest moments of his birth.

Moses was born into a cultural cauldron of anti-Semitic hatred as the Hebrew people living in Egypt were mistreated, misused, downtrodden, and enslaved. Moses entered a world defined by adversity, affliction, and despair. Pharaoh was concerned about the number of Hebrews living in Egypt, and with exceptional cruelty he mandated that '[e]very boy that is born you must throw into the Nile, but let every girl live' (Exod. 1:22). Fear and hardship colored the picture of daily living for the Hebrew people. When Jochebed, Moses' mother, discovered she was having a baby, she was certainly filled with deep anxiety.

For Moses' first three months, his sister Miriam and brother Aaron helped to keep him safe and protect their family secret. But the time would come when Moses' parents had to make a decision. As Moses grew, it would become increasingly hard to hide him. What if neighbors heard a baby's cry and began to ask questions? Imagine the long, late-night conversations when the other children were in bed and Moses' parents explored the possibilities that lay before them. Think of the tears, the concerns, the despair, and the prayers appealing to God and asking Him to wrap His arms of love and protection around Moses. Despite the dire nature of their circumstances, Moses' mother, Jochebed, came up with a plan.

At face value, however, it does not seem like much of a plan. Placing Moses in a papyrus basket and leaving him among the reeds along the banks of the Nile could easily be construed as tempting providence. Yet I imagine Jochebed was all too familiar with that section of the Nile, knew who frequented it, and left Miriam, Moses' sister, to keep watch in the prayerful hope that her presence would help to facilitate the unfolding drama.

Amidst Jochebed's strategizing activity, we can see the providence of God at work. God's providence is perhaps best defined in these words:

> God's most holy, wise, and powerful preserving and governing all his creatures and all their actions. God, the great Creator of all things, doth uphold, direct, dispose, and govern all creatures, actions, and things, from the greatest even to the least, by his most wise and holy providence, according to his infallible foreknowledge, and the free and immutable counsel of his own will, to the praise of the glory of his wisdom, power, justice, goodness, and mercy.[14]

There is no question that Jochebed was trusting in the sovereign purposes of God for her son and her family. Yet there is a considerable difference between discussing providence as an abstract concept and knowing that your son's life is at stake

---

14. http://www.opc.org/wcf.html#Chapter_05

when you place his future in the hands of God. This kind of action takes remarkable faith.

Just imagine what is going through Jochebed's mind. Think of the number of times she had outlined her plan to her daughter Miriam, explaining to her what would take place. Then she explained it again and perhaps walked her through a variety of contingencies. Now all she could do was wait and pray, and wait and pray, trusting that God would move in the heart of Pharaoh's daughter.

As Moses cries from his papyrus basket floating among the reeds, Pharaoh's daughter reacts with compassion, recognizing that this is a Hebrew baby. She is moved again when young Miriam becomes the hero of the hour by casually asking, 'Shall I go and get one of the Hebrew women to nurse the baby for you?' (Exod. 2:7).

Now it is time for Jochebed to play her part in the unfolding drama, the part of a caring, responsible, motherly figure, a slave who could be relied on. Yet she dare not show her true feelings for her son. There could be no hint of affection beyond that of a nursemaid, no betraying her heart's longing, no rejoicing at answered prayer, no great sighs of relief that God had protected her son. She could show no instant recognition of the goodness of God that henceforth she would be paid to raise her own son under the protection of Pharaoh's daughter. Moses was created for a purpose, and God was bringing together Pharaoh's daughter, with all of the privileges of a royal household and upbringing, and a little Hebrew family, who from the outside seemed to live a rather ordinary life.

As the years went by, Miriam, Aaron, and Moses developed as normal children their age. You can imagine them playing together under the kitchen table, learning to read and count, growing up together, filled with all of the dreams and hopes of an everyday family. But in the shadows was the constant reminder that one day Moses would have to leave for the palace. One day he would become a prince of Egypt. When that day came, Moses' parents would be filled with sadness, having prayed for their son, kissed him one last time, packed a bag with his few belongings, reminding him to behave, work hard, and try his best. Moses left his family home, obliged to follow a life he did not seek and did not naturally want. It was now a life with a new beginning.

When you find yourself wrestling with a new beginning not of your own choosing, it is tempting to live in the past. Moses, Miriam, and Aaron would remember tender, special moments growing up around their family home, filled with the love and affection of parents who treasured them. Such moments would remain with them the rest of their days. Jochebed would find it incredibly painful handing over Moses to be someone else's son—no longer to tuck him into bed at night, no longer hear his voice around the house or at the dinner table. Yet Jochebed and her husband, I imagine, having prayed for Moses for such a long time, committed him into the Lord's hands and understood that God had created their son for a purpose.

It would be decades before the purposes of God were clear for Moses, yet the years ahead would be years of preparation—preparing him for a deep and abiding intimacy with God; Moses was to become the one whom 'The LORD would speak to… face to face, as one speaks to a friend' (Exod. 33:11). God was preparing Moses to be the one who would receive the Ten Commandments, the leader of a nation, the great emancipator, a man who would impact the lives of millions; Moses was indeed *created for a purpose.*

Questions

1) Describe a time in your life when God delayed answering your prayers and you had to wait for His answer. What did you learn in the process?

2) As God prepared Joseph for the challenges that would come his way as one of Egypt's most influential leaders, describe how God brought about greater maturity in his life.

3) Why is abortion such a sensitive subject? What is the best way to approach it?

4) David writes about life existing in the womb. Describe what you would say to a close friend who is considering having an abortion.

5) Explain how the providence of God operates in your life. Is there comfort in the words of the apostle Paul, 'In him we were also chosen, having been predestined according to the plan of him who works out everything in conformity with the purpose of his will'?

7

A PRECIOUS PARADIGM

How precious to me are your thoughts, O God!
How vast is the sum of them!
Were I to count them,
they would outnumber the grains of sand.
When I awake, I am still with you.
(Ps. 139:17–18)

A Spontaneous Proposal?

Some time ago I experienced what most men never get to: an unsolicited proposal of marriage. I have to confess that it came as something of a surprise as the lady involved was in her early twenties, and I really did not know her that well.

I was in my local Barnes & Noble bookstore when a young barista mentioned that one of her colleagues was looking for me. I immediately suggested that it was likely Jennifer, as I had performed the marriage of Jennifer and her husband Keith three years earlier. I went on to say that, over the years, I had married two or three of the girls who worked in Barnes & Noble. Then, in a moment of unguarded spontaneity, she asked, 'Would you marry me?' In an attempt at pastoral humor, I replied, 'I am sorry. I am already married.'

As you can imagine, the young lady turned red, became flustered, smiled, and then turned a deeper shade of red. In an attempt to hide her embarrassment, she laughed a little sheepishly, and I encouraged her to share with her sister what had just transpired when she got home.

The following Sunday I told my congregation about my unsolicited proposal of marriage. After the service a male congregant in his eighties informed me, with tongue firmly in cheek, that he was heading over to Barnes & Noble that afternoon and would look forward to letting me know if he received a marriage proposal.

Funny, spontaneous moments are often moments we remember with great affection, especially if they are unexpected and appear out of nowhere. Toward the end of the opening chapter of Mark's Gospel, there is a fascinating incident that seems to appear out of nowhere, an event that is not only memorable and impactful, but also models for us the principles David highlights when he writes, 'How precious to me are your thoughts, O God! How vast is the sum of them! Were I to count them, they would outnumber the grains of sand. When I awake, I am still with you' (Ps. 139:17-18).

A Memorable Moment?

Imagine for a moment that you are Mark, a close friend of the apostle Peter and author of the Gospel. As you begin to plan and prepare the structure, content, flow, and development of your writing, how would you go about recording an account of the most extraordinary life ever lived—lived in a way that is totally engaging, warm, winsome, and utterly compelling?

As Mark begins his Gospel, he invites his readers to use their imaginations and journey back with him into the events he unfolds. It is almost as if Mark is asking you to put yourself in the disciples' situation, listening to Jesus from the earliest moments of His public ministry. Remembering what it was like to hear for the first time that deep, abiding intimacy with God is possible; realizing that God is not simply the invention of wishful thinking or inner longings, but that He is, in fact, a loving, gracious, heavenly Father who can be known personally, who impacts and transforms your soul. It was for these and many other reasons that Mark wrote his Gospel.

In order to fully grasp the unexpected events of Mark 1:35-39, it is helpful to examine the context of the passage. Mark's opening words, 'The beginning of the gospel about Jesus Christ, the Son of God,' are familiar to us; but for Mark and his readers, these opening words were of utmost importance. Mark intentionally uses language that echoes the opening words of the book of Genesis: 'In the beginning' (Gen. 1:1). He is reminding his readers that what they are about to read is so astounding that it is equivalent to the creative and transformative power of God at work in creation.

Mark then follows up his initial thoughts by indicating something new has happened, something so unprecedented that the only appropriate word he finds to capture his readers' attention is the word 'gospel.' 'Gospel' is often defined as 'good news,' yet it was also used to describe an event of staggering importance. Ancient historians described the birth of the Roman Emperor, Augustus, as a 'gospel,' meaning an event that would change world history.[1]

By using the word 'gospel,' Mark places Jesus at the epicenter of a world-changing historical event. He also goes on to emphasize that the birth of Christ is closely linked to God's previous activity, hence his quotation from the Old Testament books of Malachi and Isaiah: 'I will send my messenger ahead

---

1.   Ralph P. Martin, *Where the Action is* (Regal Books Division, Gospel Light Publications, USA, 1977), p. 10.

of you, who will prepare your way' (Mal. 3:1); and 'a voice of one calling in the desert, "Prepare the way for the LORD, make straight paths for him"' (Isa. 40:3).

As you explore Mark's opening words, it is worth remembering that he is writing to Christians who are living in the city of Rome. If we understand this, Mark's reasons for beginning the way he does make sense. The cultural pattern of first-century Rome was to look back into history and give significance and value to empires that once ruled the world, particularly the ancient Greeks. In the popular mindset of the day, looking back and exploring enduring, respected cultures was of value. By contrast, the new was often regarded with suspicion.

Mark is therefore suggesting that he is not writing about some new fad or craze, but about the fulfillment of God's purposes and plans from eternity past. This singular event of the birth of Jesus Christ would change the course of world history.

New Testament scholar William Hendrickson, in seeking to give a fuller picture of how Mark depicts Christ in his Gospel, writes: 'Mark pictures the Christ, namely, as an active, energetic, swiftly moving, warring, conquering King, a victor over the destructive forces of nature, demons and even death.'[2] We see this action in startling detail as Mark in chapter 1 presents seven major events in the early ministry of Christ. Matthew and Luke each take four chapters to describe what Mark concentrates into his opening chapter.

It comes as something of a surprise when, toward the end of chapter 1, the fast-paced, breathtaking narrative slows almost to a halt when Mark records Jesus going 'to a solitary place, where he prayed' (Mark 1:35).

---

2.   W. Hendrickson, *Mark* (Edinburgh, UK: The Banner of Truth Trust, 1981) p. 14.

A Solitary Place

Today, many of us live in a world dominated by the ubiquitous convenience of a digital playground. For some of us, it has become a mild obsession.

Recently a couple told me that when they go out to eat with other couples, they agree that all cell phones will be placed on the table, and the first person to check his phone pays for the meal. These couples are holding each other accountable for being fully present and intentionally engaged with one another.

Accustomed to life at a frantic pace, there are times when we are no longer able to discriminate between the essential and the non-essential. We find ourselves overwhelmed, overscheduled, and tired. Moments of deep intimate prayer—those times when you climb up into the lap of God and rest in Him—become little more than distant memories.

If you could find the time to sit down with Jesus and to confide in Him your deepest longings and most personal thoughts, what would you say? How would you begin that conversation? What would you ask Him? Would you look back and reminisce about events in your childhood or teenage years? Perhaps you would ask His help in getting over an event that has disturbed you deeply, or request His guidance on a major decision you are currently facing. Is there one thing above all others that you would ask Him? Prayerful moments when you get alone with God in a quiet place are essential if you are ever to develop your faith in a richer and fuller way. Jesus knew the fundamental importance of spending time with His Father and it is not a surprise that Mark features this in his opening chapter.

The first thing you notice when you engage with Mark 1:35-39 is that this event took place in Capernaum, situated sixty miles north of Jerusalem on the western shore of the Sea of Galilee. It was a sizeable town with a significant population for its day, containing both a synagogue and a Roman garrison. Capernaum was an integral part of the major trade route north, and also a tax center for the area.

When Mark informs his readers that 'Very early in the morning, while it was still dark, Jesus got up, left the house and went off to a solitary place, where he prayed,' it is important to not miss the significance of what is transpiring. The previous day had been long, busy, and demanding. Jesus had taught in the synagogue, cast out an evil spirit, and healed Simon Peter's mother-in-law. In the evening, 'The whole town gathered at the door, and Jesus healed many who had various diseases. He also drove out many demons' (Mark 1:33-34).

Traditionally, the Sabbath was a day of rest, but there was not much rest for Jesus that day. I imagine it was exhausting, leaving Him mentally and emotionally drained, especially with the number of people involved as the whole town gathered to bring Him their requests.

Most of us need a little rest and relaxation after a day of intense activity. It is surprising, then, that the next morning before the sun was up, Jesus went off to a solitary place where He prayed. The fact that it was early in the morning tells us that Jesus had to make considerable effort to secure a quiet place for uninterrupted prayer. He was clearly intentional in His action and deliberate in His approach. He sought out a place with no distractions, a solitary place where He could immerse Himself in the reality of the truth contained in David's words, 'How precious to me are your thoughts, O God!' (Ps. 139:17).

Jesus knew that in finding 'a solitary place' He was able to be alone with His Father, enjoying moments of abiding intimacy. It was a place of devotion and unimpeded adoration. Such moments birthed a wholehearted, single-minded focus on the unparalleled, matchless goodness and grace of God Himself. It was in such moments that Jesus was able to immerse Himself in God's extravagant love. Prayer was when Jesus reconnected with His Father, when He was able to be quiet, to distance Himself from the demands and priorities around Him, and to experience the reality contained within David's words, 'How precious to me are your thoughts, O God!'

A 'solitary place' is where you un-clutter your soul, where you actively reflect on the priorities in your life—the spiritual imperatives. It is where you remember who He has called you to be, a place to bring your worries and your cares—the issues that make you fearful, uncertain, and anxious—it is the place when you lay them down. In such a place you no longer have to fix everyone and everything else around you. It is where you rest in God alone. It is the place where you are reminded that prayer is both integral and indispensable in your relationship with a gracious, loving Father who knows everything about you, yet continues to love you deeply.

That solitary prayerful place is where you confide in Him your deepest longings and most personal thoughts. It is where you open your soul and seek His help in dealing with the past. It is where you seek His healing touch on incidents that continue to disturb you. It is in those moments that you wrestle with questions and uncertainties, while seeking His guiding hand on the decisions and challenges you face. This is the place to ask that one thing you most need His input on.

Moments of solitary prayer are not easy to find, yet when we are intentional and proactive in creating them, we discover that God and God alone is more than enough in such moments. There is no room for smartphones, tablets, Facebook, Instagram, or Google; there is only room for passionate, heartfelt, authentic, credible prayer. It is the place to listen and then silently utter from the deep recesses of the soul, 'How precious to me are your thoughts, O God!'

Determining Priorities

As the remainder of Mark's narrative unfolds, we discover that Simon and the other disciples search for Jesus, and when they find Him they tell Him, 'Everyone is looking for you!' (Mark 1:37). I can easily imagine Simon hastily suggesting, 'Jesus, the entire city is looking for You. You were incredible yesterday. People have never seen anything like this. The impact You had on so many was amazing. People are searching everywhere for You. Let's go back to Capernaum and make it the center of Your ministry in Galilee. People will come from all over the region. Let's go back.' Despite the seductive appeal of popularity and instant success, Jesus responds by saying, 'Let us go somewhere else, to the nearby villages so I can preach there also. That is why I have come' (Mark 1:38).

As you reflect on this passage and assess what is taking place, it gradually becomes clear that Simon and the others were preoccupied with the immediate, the now. They were caught up in the moment, but Jesus was caught up with the eternal. His time spent with His Father enabled Him to refocus on the importance of His mission, reassess the significance of His call, and realign His priorities with the eternal purposes and plans of God.

The Christian life is often shaped and fashioned in the quiet surrender of a selfless life, prayerfully submitting to the rule and reign of God each day. Such a life begins and ends in prayer. In the solitary place of prayer, we are energized and motivated to live for Him each day. Prayer shapes and refines a passion for holiness, diligence in obedience, and a desire to delight in His will. In quiet reflective prayer, faithfulness is conceived and dedication is birthed. Such faithfulness grows, thrives, and is enabled and sustained in prayer. It is submissive, engaging prayer that creates individuals who can wholeheartedly say, 'How precious to me are your thoughts, O God!'

Not What I Had in Mind!

Charlie Chaplin, the famous actor of the silent-film era, was known for being comical, charming, clownish, and highly entertaining. His little black hat, tight coat, baggy pants, and oversized shoes stole the hearts of cinemagoers in the days when silent movies were enormously popular. On one occasion, Mr. Chaplin entered a Charlie Chaplin lookalike contest and came in third. How could that happen? The judges had an image in their minds of what Charlie Chaplin looked like, and the real Charlie Chaplin did not quite fit that image.

In our study of Psalm 139, I hope there have been moments when you found yourself engaged and challenged at a level you did not initially expect. More importantly, I hope you have come to a fresh, new appreciation of the nature and character of God Himself. A prayerful focus on a passage of Scripture often surprises us by achieving what we did not imagine possible.

Exploring a psalm of the magnitude of Psalm 139 can, at times, seem a little overwhelming. As David consistently takes his readers to new and deeper levels, he encourages them not only to consider the precious nature of the thoughts of God, but also to gasp in astonishment and wonder at the comprehensive, inclusive, nurturing nature of God's thoughts: 'How vast is the sum of them! Were I to count them, they would outnumber the grains of sand.' God's thoughts reflect His character, and when David addresses God in these verses, he refers to Him as God (*El*), the Hebrew name signifying the distinctive nature of God that moves David to adoration, adulation, and awe. He considers with incredulity the vastness and magnitude of the thoughts contained within the consummate nature and character of God Himself.

The purposes and plans of God move him to realize that although God's thoughts are innumerable in nature, they are also comprehensive in design. There is no escaping them, no emptying them of their purpose and power. When David describes the moments when he awakes, refreshed from this sleep, he reminds his readers that not only do the purposes and eternal decrees of God continue to impact and shape his own life, but, more significantly, God Himself is present within His purpose and His will.

Working our way through Psalm 139, we have examined the eternal purposes and plans of God as they have manifested themselves in spectacular ways in the lives of David, Simon Peter, Joseph, and Moses. Yet for me, the eternal nature of the purposes and plans of God come to a climax in the most unexpected of places: a garden. A garden called Gethsemane.

In the first half of this chapter, we briefly explored an incident in the opening chapter of Mark's Gospel and the need for Jesus to spend some time alone with His Father in a solitary place. Toward the end of Mark's Gospel, in chapter 14, we find Jesus once again seeking a solitary place of prayer—a place where He could climb up into the lap of God and rest; a place where He could once again pour out His heart and be overwhelmed with the tender presence and reassuring love of God Himself. In chapter 14:32-41, Mark exposes his readers to one of the most sacred events in all of Scripture, and it took place in a solitary place.

Today, the Garden of Gethsemane is located at the foot of the Mount of Olives and is just under 1,300 square feet in size. Jesus and His disciples would have known the area well. Today, the garden is popular with tourists to Jerusalem, and you can hear the noises of nearby traffic and the routine life of a busy city. Yet for all of the distractions, it is relatively easy to journey back in your imagination, stand within the shadows of the trees, and watch, and listen, while seeking to understand the magnitude and significance of what took place in Gethsemane.

Subtle themes of journey, movement, purpose, and direction characterize much of Mark's Gospel: 'He traveled throughout Galilee, preaching in their synagogues' (Mark 1:39). He traveled by boat across the Sea of Galilee, journeyed with His disciples to the region of Caesarea Philippi, visited and preached in the northern territories, in Judea, across the Jordan, and in Bethphage, Bethany, and finally Jerusalem. In Mark 10:32, the 'journey' motif takes on a new emphasis when we read, 'They were on their way up to Jerusalem, with Jesus leading the way, and the disciples were astonished, while those who followed were afraid.' Jesus had clearly been the One leading the way, setting the pace, and determining the direction. Yet in the closing chapters, Mark hints that his Gospel may not finish in the way his readers had initially thought.

After a fairly tense and poignant Passover supper when Jesus institutes the sacrament of communion, highlights His forthcoming betrayal by Judas, predicts Peter's denial, and then leads the disciples to the Garden of Gethsemane, Mark's readers are left with a mounting sense of dread.

As Jesus enters the garden with His disciples, Mark informs his readers that Jesus wants Peter, James, and John close by while He seeks a solitary place to pray. It is at this point that the Gospel narrative moves to a significantly deeper level, a sacred place, a place where:

> He began to be deeply distressed and troubled. 'My soul is overwhelmed with sorrow to the point of death,' he said to them. 'Stay here and keep watch.' Going a little farther, he fell to the ground and prayed that if possible the hour might pass from him. '*Abba*, Father,' he said, 'everything is possible for you. Take this cup from me. Yet not what I will, but what you will' (Mark 14:33-36).

In full recognition of the horror, extreme violence, and emotional trauma of what would take place in the next few hours, it is no wonder that Jesus was 'deeply distressed and troubled... overwhelmed to the point of death.' It is difficult to imagine the sense of fear and terror that washed over Him when He prayed, 'everything is possible for you. Take this cup from me.' His entire life had been leading up to this point. Now the only thing that brought any sense of comfort was the realization that He was fulfilling the eternal purposes and plans of God. The understanding of what God was accomplishing by His death strengthened Jesus to persevere in the midst of the most extreme circumstances, and enabled Him to cry out, 'Yet not what I will, but what you will.'

I wonder if at Gethsemane Jesus recalled the words of David, 'How precious to me are your thoughts, O God! How vast is the sum of them!'

The Journey Continues

Several years ago, I visited Jerusalem. Like most pilgrims, I have a lasting impression of the old city's narrow, crowded streets. On one occasion while making my way through the ancient shops and busy thoroughfares, I bumped into a woman who was standing in the middle of the sidewalk praying. Surprised, I quickly apologized, but then noticed others doing the same thing. I suddenly realized I had walked into the middle of a tour group whose priest was leading them in prayer while explaining the significance of where they were and what had taken place there. We were standing at the traditional site where Simon of Cyrene was forced by Roman soldiers to carry the cross of Jesus.

In Mark 15, the journey motif continues, yet this time Jesus is not the one leading the way. 'Then they led him out to crucify him' (Mark 15:20). Mark follows up this statement by introducing his readers to Simon of Cyrene. The city of Cyrene, situated on the coast of North Africa in modern Libya, was once a busy, thriving city with a large Jewish population.

Imagine what is going on in Simon's mind. He has traveled from his country to Jerusalem, probably to take part in the Passover festivities. Walking through the narrow streets of old Jerusalem, he begins to realize that the streets are more crowded than usual. Before he can work out the reason, a Roman soldier grasps him by the arm and orders him to carry a cross. It is almost as if Simon has stumbled into what God was doing that first Good Friday.

As far as I know, we never hear of Simon again, but interestingly Mark mentions Simon's two sons, Alexander and Rufus, as if we should know who they were. A man called Rufus and his mother are later mentioned in Romans chapter 16, which may suggest that what took place that day in Jerusalem had a profound effect on the lives of Simon and his family.

As Mark continues his narrative leading up to the death of Christ, the language he uses changes. He reminds us that Jesus is no longer leading the way, but others are now seemingly in control: 'They brought Jesus to the place called Golgotha (which means the Place of the Skull)' (Mark 15:22). The very name resonates with death and dismay. 'And there they crucified him' (Mark 15:24). Mark includes no detail. He writes succinctly, using language that is cold and stark—reflective of death itself.

When we come to the point of the death of Jesus, we might expect Mark to follow his normal pattern of clipped, concise, minimalistic writing, yet that is not what he does. He records the time of Jesus' death, and then His final words—words so profound, so significant, so momentous that it is almost impossible to fully portray the significance of what took place. 'At the sixth hour darkness came over the whole land until the ninth hour. And at the ninth hour Jesus cried out in a loud voice, *"Eloi, Eloi, lema sabachthani?"* (which means, "My God, my God, why have you forsaken me?")' (Mark 15:33-34). Jesus does not call out, *'Father,* why have you forsaken me?' There is no intimate cry of *'Abba,'* no reassuring memories of 'The LORD is my Shepherd.' At that moment Jesus is experiencing the darkest and deepest of human emotions: isolation and abandonment.

It is worth remembering that throughout His life, Jesus had never known, even in the remotest sense, what it was like to be isolated from His Father. From His earliest memory as a child, the presence of God was deep and intimate, bringing an all-pervasive, supernaturally assuring peace. In each moment of every day, He was deeply aware of His Father's love and presence, profoundly in tune with His Father's will, cherishing His Father's thoughts, totally at one with Him, perhaps reassured by David's words, 'When I am awake, I am still with you' (Psalm 139:18).

At Golgotha, there was no separation of the eternal love between the Father, the Son, and the Spirit. God was no less triune at Calvary than He is elsewhere. Neither did it mean that the Father stopped loving His Son when His Son was offering Him the greatest sacrifice of all. Neither was the Son lost amidst the darkness of despair. He knew exactly what He was doing. Yet the forsakenness and abandonment that He experienced in His human nature was real and traumatic. Jesus did not merely feel forsaken. He was forsaken. When Jesus cries out to His Father, there is no response, almost as if God has not heard. God who at His baptism said, 'This is my beloved Son, with whom I am well pleased' (Mark 1:11, ESV), did not answer. There was no reply, no comforting presence, and as a tormented and lost individual He expresses the anguish of His soul.

At the moment of His greatest need, at the point of His deepest pain, the intimacy and love of His Father could not be felt, He was abandoned. Jesus cries out from the deepest recesses of His soul, 'My God, my God, why have you forsaken me?' Yet surprisingly, the worst is still to come.

When the apostle Paul writes about the experience of Jesus on the cross, he tells us, in what feels like an understated manner, that Jesus became sin for us (2 Cor. 5:21). Please try to grasp the significance of Paul's words. All of the horror, the awfulness, the mind-numbing, deceptive depravity of sin was placed on Him. A holy, perfect, righteous God, who finds sin so repulsive that He cannot countenance it, turns His back on His own Son and walks away. This is the reason Jesus cries out, 'My God, my God, why, why have you forsaken me?' It felt as though all hell had been loosed against Him. He became the object of God's perfect justice and wrath against sin. The Scriptures teach that God placed on Him the iniquity of us all (Isa. 53:6).

As we consider what Jesus experienced on the cross, we should remember that it was also an unprecedented moment for God the Father. The love, prayerful engagement and interaction between Father and Son were no more. The perfect, sinless Son of God, with whom His Father was well pleased, had become sin. The heart of God was fractured and painfully aware that He had deserted and discarded Jesus at the point of His greatest need. When we pause and consider the depths of what took place, we begin to see something of the magnitude of the love of God.

Throughout the Scriptures we are taught that sin is utterly toxic, deceptive, enticing, enslaving, and addictive. It impacts and has a tranquilizing effect on each life it touches. We see it around us today in human sex trafficking, domestic violence, and alcohol and drug addiction. It manifests itself in school and mall shootings, in terrorist attacks, and in the mayhem, violence, and in the chaos that destroys families and fractures relationships. Sin brings betrayal, hurt, pain, and devastation into the lives of everyone it comes into contact with.

At the cross, God utterly refused to sidestep sin and its effects. There was no sleight of hand, no smoke and mirrors, no pretense. At Calvary, God faced up to sin in all of its inherent evil and depravity, and defeated it forever. The One who loves us with an everlasting love made Calvary possible and is also the One who understands the devastating consequences of sin and determined that Calvary is necessary.

The apostle Paul wonderfully sums up what happened at Golgotha when he writes, 'But God demonstrates his own love for us in this: While we were still sinners, Christ died for us' (Rom. 5:8). Paul is reminding us that the love of God was extended to us not when we came to our senses and understood Christ died for us, or at the point when we repented of our sin. It was not when we were deep in prayer and searching for God; neither was it when we began to turn to Him, attend church, read the Scriptures, and develop a spiritual appetite for the things of God. Paul is clear: it was while we were still sinners who treated Him with apathy, indifference, and even contempt that He lavished His love and forgiveness upon us.

Sadly, I often come into contact with people who have, through a series of poor decisions, found themselves in a place so spiritually, emotionally, and psychologically dark that they think they can never be reached. They are in a place so devoid of hope that they believe nothing and no one can touch them. They have become so wounded and deceived by the numbing effects of their own sin that they finally believe the lie that they are a 'nobody,' always will be, and life will never get any better. The toxic, deceptive, enticing, enslaving nature of sin has captured human lives and convinced them that there is no way out. The cross tells us otherwise. It tells us that there is hope for a new beginning. When individuals surrender to the call of God on their lives, come to realize that Christ died for their sins, and place their trust in Him, transformation through the enabling power of God becomes a living reality. With this transformation comes freedom from the control of sin, and the opportunity to begin a transforming relationship with Him.

Millions across the world have had such an experience, and that is why the cross lies at the very center of Christian belief. If you have been struggling with your faith or are uncertain of your relationship with God, this chapter may well have been written just for you. Perhaps it is time to submit to His call upon your life and begin to walk with Him anew.

As Mark draws his account of the crucifixion to a close, he describes one more incident that does not include Judas or Peter or Simon of Cyrene. It involves a Roman centurion, a man for whom a crucifixion was not a new experience. Yet when this centurion heard the cry of Jesus and saw how He died, he said, 'Surely this man was the Son of God!' (Mark 15:39). It is more than a little surprising that these words do not come from the high priest or a leading rabbi—not even from a loyal disciple—but from a Roman centurion, the man in charge of the execution squad. It is almost as if he also stumbles into what God is doing.

At what should have been the lowest point of the gospel narrative, the centurion discovers for himself what Mark announced at the beginning of his Gospel: 'The gospel of Jesus Christ, the Son of God.' Here at the site of the crucifixion, it is the centurion who truly realizes what is taking place.

We have come a long way in this chapter and journeyed far. We began by examining the words of David in Psalm 139: 'How precious to me are your thoughts, O God! How vast is the sum of them! Were I to count them, they would outnumber the grains of sand. When I awake, I am still with you' (Ps. 139:17-18). Those words led us to explore the precious nature of God's thoughts manifest in the significance of the opening words of Mark's Gospel, followed by the significance of Jesus' seeking a solitary place to pray, and the importance and crucial nature of prayer.

We then ventured into the penultimate chapter of Mark, into Gethsemane where Jesus prayerfully wrestles with the thoughts and plans of God displayed in His eternal purposes for humanity. And finally we traveled the road to Golgotha, where the purposes of God were fulfilled at the cross in an act so selfless, so utterly comprehensive in its nature, that history held its breath. It was at Calvary that God exposed us to a love that is long enough to last throughout all eternity. Millennia cannot weary it. Denial, betrayal, and apathy cannot empty it of its power. This love is so high that infinity cannot encompass it and so deep that human depravity can never exhaust it.

The journey you have been on is not for the fainthearted. When you come to a new appreciation of the transforming love of Christ, recognizing that He is able to do immeasurably more than you can ask or imagine, you find yourself, as we discovered in the opening chapter, seeking to be submissive to His will, challenged by His holiness, nourished by His truth, and moved to worship Him, who alone is 'eternal, infinite, immeasurable, incomprehensible, omnipotent...'[3] It is no wonder that you find your heart rejoicing when you read David's words, 'How precious to me are your thoughts, O God! How vast is the sum of them! Were I to count them, they would outnumber the grains of sand. When I awake, I am still with you' (Ps. 139:17-18).

---

3. James Bulloch, *The Scots Confession, a Modern Translation* (Edinburgh, Scotland: Saint Andrew Press, 1991), p. 3.

Questions

1) Describe what David means when he writes, 'How precious to me are your thoughts, O God.' How important are the thoughts of God to you in your daily routine?

2) When Jesus seeks out a 'solitary place to pray,' He is intentional about spending time in prayer. Why was prayer so important to Jesus in the midst of a busy and demanding day? Explain what takes place when you pray.

3) Has there been a time when God unexpectedly answered your prayers? Explain what happened.

4) When we read in Mark's Gospel of Simon of Cyrene (Mark 15:21) and the Roman centurion (Mark 15:39), it seems as if they both stumbled into what God was doing. Describe a time when you had a similar experience.

5) David writes, 'How precious to me are your thoughts, O God! How vast the sum of them!' Describe the magnitude of what took place at the cross.

8

RESPONDING TO THE
UNTHINKABLE

If only you would slay the wicked, O God!
Away from me, you bloodthirsty men!
They speak of you with evil intent;
your adversaries misuse your name.
Do I not hate those who hate you, O LORD,
and abhor those who rise up against you?
I have nothing but hatred for them;
I count them my enemies.
(Ps. 139:19–22)

Wars and Rumors of War

David's words in this section are initially unexpected and jarring: 'If only you would slay the wicked, O God! Away from me, you bloodthirsty men! … Do I not hate those who hate you, O LORD…? I have nothing but hatred for them; I count them my enemies' (Ps. 139:19-22). These sentiments stand in stark contrast to the focus of the psalm up to this point. Not only do his words strike you as harsh and strident but they also raise a number of significant questions.

Is David suggesting that you should pray for the destruction of those you personally dislike? Is he giving vent to some kind of private vindictiveness, expressing malice and unrestrained hatred? Is he modeling animosity and disdain for those he disapproves of?

Touring Germany in 2014, I visited Buchenwald, a Nazi concentration camp near the town of Weimar in east central Germany. The camp first opened in July 1937. It was one of the first, and at that time the largest, of the concentration camps that followed the opening of Dachau in 1934. Prisoners from various countries in Europe were detained in Buchenwald— Jews, Slavs, Poles, and religious and political prisoners, along with criminals and prisoners of war. Estimates based on documents found in the camp suggest that a total of 240,000 prisoners were held in captivity, and approximately 56,545 died in Buchenwald by the time the camp was liberated by the US army in April 1945.

The camp visit was a sobering and moving experience. Up to this point, our tour group had been constantly questioning our patient tour guide about the historical significance of the castles, cathedrals, and ancient towns we visited. In Buchenwald, however, not much was said. It was difficult to process the unrestrained wickedness that had taken place there. The barbed wire, guard towers, grainy photographs of emaciated, skeletal-looking inmates, and camp crematorium told a horrific story. General Dwight D. Eisenhower, the supreme commander of the Allied Forces, wrote of Buchenwald, 'Nothing has ever shocked me as much as that sight.'[1]

Encountering evil is indeed a somber and sobering experience. It is difficult to get your mind around the depravity that took place at Buchenwald. Yet it was only one of approximately 42,500 ghettos and camps throughout Europe.[2] Estimates suggest that 15 to 20 million people died in captivity under the Third Reich.

1. https://en.wikipedia.org/wiki/Buchenwald_concentration_camp.
2. https://www.nytimes.com/2013/03/03/sunday-review/the-holocaust-just-got-more-shocking.html.

It is difficult to determine David's mindset in writing Psalm 139 or the exact context, yet we know he described his enemies as 'wicked' and 'bloodthirsty,' with 'evil intent.' Buchenwald Concentration Camp and so many others demonstrated the necessity of standing up against those who are wicked, bloodthirsty, and have evil intent.

As Israel's king, David was responsible for the safety of his people. On more than one occasion, he had to decide how to respond when evil threatened to overwhelm his nation and its people.

St. Augustine (AD 354-430), bishop of Hippo in Numidia in Roman North Africa, is considered by many the father of systematic theology, first-class philosopher, prolific author of more than 200 books, and the most influential Church Father of the Patristic Era (AD 100-500). Even today, Augustine's Principles of Just-War Theory influence our decisions regarding resisting those who have evil intent.

Augustine's Principles of Just-War Theory include the following:

- A justifiable war can only be entered into by a legitimate government and not by independent groups or individuals.

- A just war needs to be in response to a wrong inflicted upon a nation or people, and its required objective is to correct the action taken by a hostile group.

- There must be a distinct possibility of a favorable outcome; war should be rejected on the basis if there is no possibility of success.

- The intended objective of a just war is to re-establish peace, and if possible, to exceed the peace that existed before hostilities began. 'We do not seek peace in order to be at war, but we go to war that we may have peace. Be peaceful, therefore, in warring, so that you may vanquish those whom you war against, and bring them to the prosperity of peace.'[3] The proper intent is a primary focus of a just war.

- The use of military force must always be in proportion to the casualties suffered. Disproportionate force must be avoided.

- The distinction between civilians and military combatants must be recognized and sustained. The use of force against civilians is to be avoided. The deaths of civilians can only be justified when they are considered unavoidable victims of an attack on a strategic military target.

- A just war can only be fought after all peaceful options are exhausted; armed conflict is used as a last resort.

Augustine's principles have stood the test of time and continue to be used today when it comes to considering the moral reasons for going to war, engaging in military combat, and deciding how to treat a former enemy once the objectives of the war have been met.

Let's explore further the significance of David's words. What do the Scriptures teach you to do when you have been personally attacked? How should you respond to those responsible?

In a variety of places throughout the Psalms, we find what have been classified as imprecatory psalms. These passages call down the judgment of God and express hatred for the enemies of God. Examples are Psalms 10:15; 28:4; 31:17-18; 35:4-6; 40:14-15; 58:6-11; 69:22-28; 109:6-15; 139:19-22; and 140:9-10. Biblical scholars have produced numerous interpretations on the exegetical and ethical significance of these psalms. Bear in mind that 'hatred' can fall into the category of moral repugnance, as in the case of Buchenwald concentration camp, rather than a desire for personal vengeance.

---

3. http://www.thelatinlibrary.com/imperialism/readings/aquinas.html.

Look again at the fundamental question that dominates this section, Psalm 139:19-22: How should we respond when we are personally attacked? Do we find ourselves identifying with David, 'I have nothing but hatred for them; I count them my enemies'?

Why Forgive?

On Wednesday evening, 17 June 2015, an event took place that shocked and appalled those who heard about it an hour later on national news. At Mother Emmanuel AME church in Charleston, South Carolina, nine people were shot and killed by twenty-one-year-old Dylann Roof. Toward the end of the midweek Bible Study during a time of prayer, Roof, who had joined the group earlier that evening, produced a handgun and began shooting. He reloaded five times.

When Roof was arrested and appeared in court a few days later, family members and friends who had lost parents, grandparents, and, in one case, an adult child, spoke these words:

'I forgive you. You took something very precious away from me. I will never get to talk to her ever again. I will never be able to hold her again, but I forgive you, and have mercy on your soul... You hurt me. You hurt a lot of people. If God forgives you, I forgive you.' *(Nadine Collier, daughter of victim Ethel Lance)*

'We welcomed you Wednesday night in our Bible study with welcome arms. You have killed some of the most beautiful people that I know. Every fiber in my body hurts and I'll, I'll never be the same. Tywanza Sanders was my son. But Tywanza Sanders was my hero. Tywanza was my hero... May God have mercy on you.' *(Felicia Sanders, mother of Tywanza Sanders)*

'That was my sister, and I'd like to thank you on behalf of my family for not allowing hate to win. For me, I'm a work in progress. And I acknowledge that I am very angry. But one thing that DePayne always enjoined in our family… is she taught me that we are the family that love built. We have no room for hating, so we have to forgive. I pray God on your soul.' *(Sister of DePayne Middleton-Doctor)*

'I would just like him to know that, to say the same thing that was just said: I forgive him and my family forgives him. But we would like him to take this opportunity to repent. Repent. Confess. Give your life to the One who matters most: Christ. So that He can change him and change your ways, so no matter what happens to you, you'll be okay.' *(Relative of Myra Thompson)[4]*

The family and friends who attended the arraignment of Dylann Roof were speaking on behalf of lost loved ones who had been murdered. This senseless act of violence was not the spontaneous act of a madman, but rather the action of a mind focused on evil intent, carnage, and violence, a mind intoxicated with a grandiose understanding of self-importance. This malicious, vicious, premeditated, pernicious act treated the victims with utter contempt and disdain. Yet somehow family members and friends were able to extend forgiveness.

Hopefully you never will find yourself in similar circumstances, but you may have other significant personal challenges in your life. You may have experienced an acrimonious and difficult divorce, or been involved in a close friendship which has fractured and turned sour, and horrible and hurtful things have been said. How do you respond when you discover your spouse has been involved in an affair and left

---

4.   https://www.washingtonpost.com/news/post-nation/wp/2015/06/19/
     hate-wont-win-the-powerful-words-delivered-to-dylann-roof-by-
     victims-relatives/?utm_term =.4910f9e03bd9

you betrayed, belittled, and traumatized? How do you recover from the horrors of incest or domestic violence?

Attempting to move on with your life when you have been emotionally and psychologically wounded is difficult, especially when you hurt so badly that the pain never seems to leave you. Each day you wrestle with bitterness, despair, and despondency, continuing to relive past events in your mind, thinking about what you would really like to do to the person who has hurt you. You feel angry all the time, powerless to take any action, uncertain what to do. Emotionally you are at your breaking point.

An individual going through such an extreme experience would understandably feel that 'I have nothing but hatred for them; I count them my enemies' (Ps. 139:22). Yet despite the pain involved, we also need to explore the role forgiveness plays when responding to emotional and traumatic wounds.

In Luke's Gospel, in a passage which highlights the importance of forgiveness, we read that one of Jesus' disciples asked Him, 'Lord, teach us to pray' (Luke 11:1-4). Given that the disciple could have asked Jesus any number of questions or sought His help and insight with a multiplicity of issues, why would a disciple ask Jesus to teach him how to pray? Could it be that the disciple saw the link between Jesus' prayer life and how He lived out His faith each day? The link was evident between His prayers and His ability to live a life fashioned and molded by honesty, integrity, character, and holiness. The disciple observed the link between prayer and living an authentic credible lifestyle amidst the distractions and demands of daily living.

Back in chapter 7, we noticed that after an incredibly busy day Jesus knew He needed to reconnect with His Father (Mark 1:35-39) and as he did so the disciples could see in that event and in several others that prayer was not so much an activity, but rather a central part of His identity. Could it be that the disciples wanted to learn how to pray in order that they could live in a similar manner? As Jesus taught the disciples how to pray (Matt. 6:9-13), He includes, 'Forgive us our debts as we also have forgiven our debtors,' highlighting for them the innate necessity of forgiveness.

Consider what forgiveness means, and what it does not mean. Forgiveness on a personal level is not about approving or excusing or justifying another's actions. Neither is it pretending to be unharmed or repressing what took place. It is not refusing to deal with what happened, and neither is it pretending it doesn't matter.

Forgiveness involves a conscious choice to release someone from a wrong inflicted upon you. It means intentionally releasing a person from a debt or obligation. Forgiveness is the conscious decision by the wronged person to release the other person, whether or not reconciliation takes place, and whether or not that person ever does business or associates with you or becomes friends again.

Forgiveness can be offered on either a *unilateral* or a *transactional* basis. Unilateral forgiveness takes place when you forgive someone who has not sought forgiveness. If you are waiting for someone to ask for forgiveness and that person never apologizes, shows remorse, or says, 'I am sorry,' it may be that you are emotionally and psychologically being held hostage to what has taken place.

At the death of Stephen in the New Testament book of Acts, we read, 'While they were stoning him, Stephen prayed, "Lord Jesus, receive my spirit." Then he fell on his knees and cried out, "Lord, do not hold this sin against them"' (Acts 7:59-60). Stephen displayed Christlike character in the most extreme circumstances by extending unilateral forgiveness.

If you have experienced deep and enduring pain at the hands of a person who is now dead or is no longer involved in your life, and you are waiting for that person to express sorrow for what was done, you may find that you are being held hostage to what has occurred. What took place may be dominating your life—the first thing you think of each morning and the last thing you think of each night. Genuine forgiveness can free you. Through unilateral forgiveness, you take the initiative, extend forgiveness, and make a conscious effort to move on.

Transactional forgiveness, however, involves a different approach. When a person recognizes the pain he or she has caused, confesses, requests forgiveness, and demonstrates repentance for the wrong that has been inflicted, the door to reconciliation is open.

If you are seeking to authentically live out your faith amidst deep and personal pain while struggling to understand the role of forgiveness, remember that the Bible repeatedly encourages us to forgive. 'Bear with each other and forgive one another if any of you has a grievance against someone. Forgive as the Lord forgave you' (Col. 3:13). 'Be kind and compassionate to one another, forgiving each other, just as in Christ God forgave you' (Eph. 4:32). The apostle Paul is reminding us that God has finally and fully forgiven our sins against Him. Because of His extravagant love and unrestrained grace, He has unilaterally forgiven us.

Notice that God did not forgive us when we initially expressed an interest in Him, began to attend church, or first prayed. Neither did He wait until we apologized and expressed our sorrow for our sins. It was 'while we were still sinners, Christ died for us' (Rom. 5:8). God unilaterally demonstrated His love for us at Calvary. He took the initiative. He reached out to us.

You may be saying, 'I agree with you, that is what the Scriptures teach. But if you knew what I have been through, you would not glibly suggest that I take the initiative and extend forgiveness. I have been so badly wounded I am not sure I will ever get over it. What do I do with the pain from wounds that feel infected? I was betrayed, verbally attacked. It was malicious and vicious, and, quite frankly, I want revenge. I want everyone to know exactly what happened, what those people did to me, what kind of people they are.' You may, in fact, find yourself identifying with David's words: 'I have nothing but hatred for them; I count them my enemies' (Ps. 139:22).

When you have been emotionally wounded, it is natural that you want the pain to go away. Yet be careful to not identify only with the wounds and the associated pain. You may be in danger of focusing only on what has taken place and not on the healing and wholeness required to become healthy again.

When something or someone reminds you of what happened, the pain increases, and you find yourself continually focusing on the wounds and the hurt you can't get past. You may be in danger of being held hostage to your emotions, your circumstances, or a relationship that no longer exists. Under these circumstances, sin reaches into your life, touches you where you are fragile and vulnerable, dominates your thought processes, and controls you emotionally. You may find it difficult to move forward with your life because of the level of emotional pain, anger, and sense of impotence. Yet it is possible to break free from the anxiety and despondency you are experiencing and begin the healing process.

Jesus teaches us to pray, 'Forgive us our debts as we also have forgiven our debtors.' Consistently refusing to extend forgiveness is best summed up in the old saying, 'A lack of forgiveness is like drinking poison in the hope that the other person will pass away.'

In the story of Joseph, which we explored in earlier chapters, Joseph's brothers hated him so intensely that they physically attacked him, planned to kill him, and eventually sold him into slavery in Egypt, explaining to their father that he had been killed. Many years later, when he had become one of the most powerful men in the nation, Joseph met up with his brothers, told them to go home and let his father know that he was alive and well. He did not say, 'Go and tell my father what you did.' Joseph had every reason to seek revenge, yet he refused to do so. He offered unilateral forgiveness because he did not want to be held captive by the past or allow it to determine his future.

But before we explore how to actively move on with your life when you have been badly wounded, there is one other area worth addressing.

Facing the Unthinkable

Some time ago, over an eighteen-month period, several people I knew experienced a suicide in their family. The questions raised were so prevalent that I decided to explore the topic of suicide with my congregation on a Sunday morning, examining what the Bible teaches about suicide, and how to respond to the overwhelming emotions when someone you know takes their own life.

Back in 2011, just before 2:00pm on August 23, I was standing beside my desk in the church office when I felt the building shudder. It came as such a surprise I walked over to the window and looked out into the parking lot, as I was sure a truck had collided with the building. About ten minutes later I began receiving emails that there had been a 5.8 magnitude earthquake 497 miles away, in Washington, DC. The Washington Monument, Union Station, and the National Cathedral all required extensive repairs, costing $35 million for the monument and cathedral alone.

The secondary effects of an earthquake are sometimes greater than the actual event: fires from broken gas mains, flooding from ruptured water lines, broken electrical and telecommunication connections. In a matter of minutes, the once familiar is in ruins and unrecognizable.

When a family experiences the debilitating sadness of a suicide, it devastates those who are at its epicenter and brings chaos and confusion to many others as well. It has the effect of shaking the stable foundations of our lives, with aftereffects and shock waves that are felt for a long time to come.

During 2015, a total of 44,193 Americans took their own lives. *The Washington Post* reported in April 2016 that the US suicide rate had surged to a thirty-year high. Suicide rates had increased in every age group except older adults.[5] Each suicide leaves behind on average six to ten survivors—husbands, wives, parents, children, siblings, other family members, and close friends.

Though all deaths are tragic, suicide affects us differently than deaths in car accidents or terminal illnesses. Counselors call death by suicide a 'complicated grief.' Family members not only grieve the loss of the loved one; they must also face the trauma of the suicide, which often involves wrestling with a sense of denial, abandonment, anger, guilt, and shame. Families need to understand that these are entirely normal. Enabling family members to mourn, grieve, and lament is an important step, especially in the early stages of the healing process.

More than other deaths, suicides raise the question of *why*. Why did she do it? Why didn't we see this coming? In other situations, we can clearly identify the cause: a drunk driver or a terminal disease. But with a suicide, the victim is responsible

---

5. https://www.nytimes.com/2016/04/22/health/us-suicide-rate-surges-to-a-30-year-high.html

for the death, not some external force, yet we cannot ask the person why they took their own life.

Asking *why* is not always a search for answers. It can also be a search for comfort, with the assumption that having answers will ease our grief and pain. But the questions are often unanswerable, and we must come to grips with the possibility that we will never know why it happened.

The dominant question regularly asked by relatives is: 'Could I have done anything to prevent it?' After a suicide, families often replay various scenarios in their minds, wondering if they could have prevented it: 'If only we had done something differently.' 'If only we had come home in time.' 'If only we had talked to him earlier that evening.' 'If only we had texted or phoned.'

When family members blame themselves, survivor's guilt is common. Usually, however, family members eventually reach a point of acceptance and realize that their loved one chose to die. Despite the debilitating sadness and grief, they realize they couldn't do anything about it and they are not at fault.

Another question usually comes up, particularly among people of faith: 'Why didn't God prevent this?' There are no easy answers to this question, and a logical, rational explanation to families who are emotionally wounded and grieving rarely helps. It is, however, worth remembering that God grants to us, as an innate part of our humanity, the ability to make choices, and this involves the risk that from time to time we will make bad choices. If we choose to smoke, we may be diagnosed with lung cancer. If we choose to drive without a seatbelt, we may die in a car accident. If we choose to take drugs, we may die from drug addiction. Central to our humanity is the ability to make choices and then living with the consequences of our choices. This does not mean that God doesn't care about us or our loved ones. In the well-known story of Lazarus in John's

Gospel (John 11:1-44), we read that Jesus wept at the tomb of Lazarus. He likewise stands with us and grieves over the loss of life and accompanying pain and anguish we experience when someone we love is no longer with us.

Throughout Scripture, God comforts the grieving and brokenhearted. He recognizes and empathizes with our suffering, grief, and loss. When we wonder where God is in the midst of our grief, He stands right beside us, grieving along with us.

Warning Signs

When someone we know takes her own life we often ask ourselves, 'Were there warning signs? If so, what were they?' The warning signs of suicide often include prolonged depression and despondency, detachment or withdrawal, a loss of interest in normal activities, giving away possessions, suicidal thoughts or fantasies, and suicide attempts. If you see these warning signs in a loved one, you need to seek help. Talk to her about what she is experiencing. Ask how he is feeling, and specifically ask if he has thought about taking his own life. Don't worry that asking someone about suicide might give that person ideas; many depressed people are already thinking about suicide and desperately want someone to talk to about it. A suicide attempt is a cry for help. If needed, ask a pastor or counselor for help, or call a suicide hotline or even the police. The number-one cause of suicide is untreated depression. If you see signs, seek help.

Children's Perspective

When children experience suicide in a family, they also deal with a range of emotions. They can feel forsaken and think that the person who died did not love them. Children have a tendency to believe that somehow the death is their fault, or that somehow they will also die soon, or that someone else they love will die soon. They may be anxious about who will take care of them.

Amidst the confusion of emotions, children will face moments of deep sadness, embarrassment, confusion, anger, and an anticipated sense of loneliness. Children who go through a suicide in the family need an adult to be fully engaged with them, listen to them, empathize with them, and talk with them, explaining that it is acceptable to feel the way they do. Reassure them that you love them and will continue to love them and be there for them. Try if at all possible to treat them exactly the same way you always have. Routine, stability, love, and reassurance are critical at this point. Children need to know that in the midst of the chaos and perplexing emotions, you will be there for them.

'For I am convinced...'

Seeking to gently and lovingly answer questions with wisdom and insight amidst the tragic and devastating circumstances of suicide is not easy. People often ask, 'Is the person who has taken his or her life in heaven?'

Many people consider suicide 'the unforgivable sin,' believing that those who take their lives cannot be in heaven because they died with the stain of sin upon their souls. Others, however, see hope.

The New Testament book of Romans, the primary book for Christian truth and doctrine, is considered by many to be the apostle Paul's *magnum opus,* a masterpiece of singular distinction. The book highlights the eternal and transforming nature of the extravagant love and exquisite grace of God in

Christ. It is easy to run out of superlatives when attempting to accurately and adequately describe the book of Romans.

If you are seeking to grow deeper in your understanding of the extravagant love of God personified in the gospel, you must regularly engage with the text of Romans. This epistle equips you for the day-to-day challenges and contingencies that come your way, and helps to shape and fashion your priorities as you seek to live out your faith amidst the joy and blessings of the Christian life.

If Romans is the greatest epistle of the New Testament, chapter eight is arguably its greatest chapter. It is one of the best-known chapters in all of Scripture. From its opening words to its completion, it contains approximately 958 words in most English translations and can be read in around seven minutes.

Yet, as a passage, it has been metaphorically described as a series of mountain peaks that force its readers to climb higher and higher as they make their ascent from one spectacular spiritual viewpoint to another. It also contains a number of places where you can rest for a moment, breathe deeply, and be refreshed and renewed as you look back down the trail you have just climbed. It is difficult to imagine a more inspiring, exhilarating, thought-provoking plateau than Romans chapter eight.

Paul begins and ends the chapter by writing in clear, unambiguous terms that are theologically profound and foundational to our understanding of the very heart of the gospel. He opens with, 'There is now no condemnation for those who are in Christ Jesus' (Rom. 8:1), and closes the chapter with the powerful reminder that nothing can 'separate us from the love of God that is in Christ Jesus our Lord' (Rom. 8:38-39). Paul is reminding his original readers, and us, that regardless of what we are facing—personal fears, deep insecurities, feelings of uncertainty—God, in His redemptive love, has secured our eternal salvation in and through what Christ accomplished on the cross. In so doing, Paul emphasizes for us that the love of Christ is eternal in nature, and entirely sufficient to fully accomplish our salvation.

In discussing suicide, we must recognize that taking a life is an extremely serious sin, an act that should never be minimized or marginalized. When an individual takes a life, that individual is accountable to God for that act.

People who commit suicide, however, are often in a place so dark and so painful that they are no longer in their right mind. The intense pain they are struggling with is, for them, simply unbearable. Over 90 percent of those who tragically take their own lives exhibit signs of mental illness. It is, therefore, worth recognizing that just as God will not punish an individual for being physically ill with a terminal illness, He will not punish an individual for wrestling with a mental illness.

Notice again the incredible reassuring promises of God toward the end of Romans 8: 'For I am convinced that neither death nor life, neither angels nor demons, neither the present nor the future, nor any powers, neither height nor depth, nor anything else in all creation, will be able to separate us from the love of God that is in Christ Jesus our Lord' (Romans 8:38-39).

The Scriptures repeatedly remind us that Christ did not simply make salvation *possible*, but rather He made it *actual*. The promises of God are not about the mere possibility of salvation. They do not simply focus on potential, probability, or feasibility. The love of God contained within the gospel is clear, definitive, exhaustive, and absolute. When we respond to the grace of God offered in and through His eternal love, *nothing* can separate us from the love of Christ. We know this because our salvation is not predicated on something we have done, but on what Christ has done at Calvary.

Scripture is clear: God will not abandon us at the point of greatest need. He will not walk away from us or desert us. The circumstances of a person's death do not, and will not, determine his or her eternal salvation. It is your relationship with Christ that determines your salvation. It is His eternal love for you and your response to His love that matters most. When Christ lavishes His undeserved love upon you, He will not then abandon you or let you go.

Yet you may be tempted to think that individuals can lose their faith. Individuals do, of course, continue to sin after they enter into a relationship with Christ, and can fall badly, but the Scriptures do not teach that we can fall totally and finally. David, whose life we have explored in several chapters, sadly surrendered to the seductive, tranquilizing, enslaving power of sin when he committed adultery with Bathsheba and then arranged for her husband's death (2 Sam. 11). We will examine this episode in the next chapter. Yet despite hurting himself and those around him, David is eventually restored to the Lord. Simon Peter, one of Jesus' closest friends, also sinned badly, but not finally or completely, as the love of Christ also restored his relationship (see Luke 22; John 21).

At the heart of God's redemptive purposes is His refusal to surrender us to the circumstances of this life or to abandon us to the destructive forces of our own sin. Romans chapter 8 and other Scripture passages teach us that the salvation of God is not partial, but complete. In the midst of the tears and the pain of a death in the family, as we wrestle with the 'what-ifs' and the 'if-onlys' compounded by the mind-numbing grief of losing a loved one, we can hold on to the promises of God. 'For I am convinced that neither death nor life, neither angels nor demons, neither the present nor the future, nor any powers, neither height nor depth, nor anything else in all creation, will be able to separate us from the love of God that is in Christ Jesus our Lord' (Rom. 8:38-39).

It is the equipping and enabling grace of God that enables us to get through the most difficult of circumstances. Resting in His comforting presence allows us to move forward, entirely reliant on His love and dependent on His grace.

Now What?

Earlier in this chapter we looked at what it means to offer forgiveness when you have been emotionally and psychologically wounded and are struggling with resentment, despair, and despondency, continuing to relive past events in your mind. In such circumstances, it is difficult to get past the events or the person who has treated you so badly. You can identify with David's words, 'I have nothing but hatred for them; I count them my enemies' (Ps. 139:22).

If you find yourself identifying with David's words, you may be asking what further steps you need to take. In addition to offering forgiveness, how do you move toward healing and wholeness, putting past events behind you?

Recently I was in a restaurant with my wife and son for lunch. High up on the wall, a large-screen television was tuned in to an international soccer match. Tens of thousands of excited fans made it clear that it was a thrilling game. On the other side of the restaurant, a second large-screen television aired an NFL game. Once again the fans' cheers and yells told us they were captivated with the action. Just behind me a third screen broadcast news headlines; occasionally people would glance up to follow the breaking news.

In his epistle to the Philippians, the apostle Paul reminds his readers in the opening chapter that he has been imprisoned for his faith and is about to go on trial for his life. Yet in the final chapter he writes, 'Do not be anxious about anything, but in everything, by prayer and petition, with thanksgiving, present your requests to God. And the peace of God, which transcends all understanding, will guard your hearts and your minds in Christ Jesus' (Phil. 4:6-7).

Lest you think that Paul is merely spouting platitudes and does not know what he is talking about, please remember the context in which he is writing. He is being closely watched by imperial guards in a Roman prison cell. It is almost as if he is inviting us to keep an eye on three screens of a developing narrative. The first screen reminds us of the extreme challenge Paul is facing; the second screen focuses on the importance of making prayer a priority if you are ever to move forward and mature in your faith; the third screen draws you into recognizing the reality of the peace of God that transcends all understanding.

As you read Paul's words 'Do not be anxious about anything' (Phil. 4:6), you may be thinking, 'That is impossible. My anxiety level has been so high recently that I cannot imagine it ever becoming less. I have tried so many times to put these painful issues out of my mind.' Yet Paul is confined in prison, facing the pressures of an imperial trial, and is still able to write, 'but in everything, by prayer and petition, with thanksgiving, present your requests to God' (Phil. 4:6).

When you find yourself in a seemingly impossible situation, remember that you have choices. On a practical basis, you can learn to rein in and control your thoughts, so they do not control you. Your responsibility mentally is not to focus on the things you have no control over, but to acknowledge the challenges you face and then hand them over entirely to the Lord. This will allow you to focus on the things you can control, leaving the rest with Him.

Leaving your prayer requests with the Lord is not easy, yet it must be done. Discipline your mind so that when you bring your prayer requests to God, you leave them with Him. Begin by prayerfully acknowledging the difficulty of what you are attempting to do: 'Father, I can't deal with this situation anymore. It is dominating my life and defining who I am. Enable me to hand it over and leave it with You. Help me to not get caught up with things outside of my control, things I can do nothing about. Allow me to trust You for healing and wholeness, and then to move on.'

When you engage God in this manner, remember what God has promised: 'And the peace of God, which transcends all understanding, will guard your hearts and your minds in Christ Jesus' (Phil. 4:7). Encountering and depending on the supernatural peace of God amidst complex and difficult challenges is a remarkable experience, one worth striving for.

The apostle Paul, however, is not finished with his practical advice. He encourages you to actively engage your mind by focusing on 'Whatever is true, whatever is noble, whatever is right, whatever is pure, whatever is lovely, whatever is admirable—if anything is excellent or praiseworthy—think about such things... put it into practice. And the God of peace will be with you' (Phil. 4:8-9).

Paul is teaching his readers to allow their minds to concentrate on what they can control and to prayerfully think on 'whatever is true.' This should motivate you to focus on the truthfulness and reality of God's covenant love and goodness toward you. The Scriptures teach that the covenant love of God is a strong, personal, unbreakable bond that He will never back away from, despite the cost to Himself.

Paul's instructions move on to inspire us to consider 'whatever is noble.' Prayerfully give thanks for the extraordinary blessing of the people in your life who genuinely, deeply love you—

children and grandchildren, parents, siblings, and friends who consistently care for you, want the very best for you, pray for you, and encourage you.

Paul adds a reminder to concentrate on 'whatever is right.' Here he is urging us to cultivate those Christlike attributes of integrity, honesty, transparency, godly character, and holiness. If we are to be the individuals God is calling us to be, our lifestyle must involve intentional Christlike decisions, choices that reflect His character as we seek to follow Him.

Paul then includes 'whatever is pure,' highlighting the importance of purity in our thought processes, in our interactions with others, and in what we choose to feed our heart and soul. Elsewhere he writes, 'We take captive every thought to make it obedient to Christ' (2 Cor. 10:5). Purity matters in every aspect of our daily lives. It is never to be considered optional.

As you face the challenges before you and seek to apply biblical principles to living out your faith each day, it may be helpful to remember three simple words: *Reassess, Refocus, Redirect*. In light of all that we have explored in this chapter, prayerfully now:

- *Reassess* the quality of your relationship with Him;
- *Refocus* your daily priorities in order to follow Him;
- *Redirect* your life each day in light of His love for you.

When you actively engage with God at an intimate level and are able to extend forgiveness, He equips you for life by removing the heartache and pain of emotionally inflicted wounds and the accompanying sense of anger. He then brings peace, renewal, and refreshment as He reminds you that you are infinitely loved by Him. When you 'think about such things,' you discover that you can rest and have confidence that He will enable you to face pain, process it, and move on.

And remember, you don't need to get revenge on the people who may have hurt you. The Lord will deal with them in His time and in His way. Neither do you need to protect your reputation. He can do that. What others think of you ultimately does not matter. Only what He thinks of you matters.

Hand over the painful situation to God, forgive, forget, and begin to move on. Then healing and wholeness 'and the God of peace will be with you' (Phil. 4:9).

Questions

1) David describes his adversaries as 'wicked' and 'bloodthirsty' with 'evil intent' (Ps. 139:19-20). How should you respond to those who behave in this manner?

2) If you have experienced a time when you were traumatized by an event or a personal attack, and you found it difficult to get over the pain involved, how did you respond? Did you find yourself identifying with David's words, 'I have nothing but hatred for them; I count them my enemies' (Ps. 139:22)?

3) Explain why forgiveness is so important in the life of the Christian.

4) Why is suicide considered a 'complicated grief'? How does Romans 8:35-39 help?

5) The apostle Paul writes, 'Do not be anxious about anything, but in everything, by prayer and petition, with thanksgiving, present your requests to God. And the peace of God, which transcends all understanding, will guard your hearts and your minds in Christ Jesus' (Phil. 4:6-7). Explain the steps involved in reducing your level of anxiety.

6) Paul writes, 'whatever is true, whatever is noble, whatever is right, whatever is pure, whatever is lovely, whatever is admirable—if anything is excellent or praiseworthy—think about such things' (Phil. 4:8). How do these principles help you focus on what you can control rather than focusing on what you can't control?

9

CULTIVATING A
WILLINGNESS TO SEARCH

Search me, O God, and know my heart;
test me and know my anxious thoughts.
See if there is any offensive way in me,
and lead me in the way everlasting.
(Ps. 139:23-24)

'Meanwhile...'

Throughout this book I have sought to explore with you the hidden depths of Psalm 139. In doing so I hope there have been moments when you have been moved to prayer, come to a fresh appreciation of the character and nature of God, and discovered new levels of intimacy in your relationship with Him. Such experiences, as you have no doubt discovered, are not for the fainthearted.

When you begin to engage with God at a new level, there is a price to be paid. It is not easy to ask fearless, searching, spiritual questions at a deeper level, and although it may be painful and intensely personal, it is always a healthy experience. In this final chapter, the probing personal questions raised in Psalm 139 are no less frequent as David encourages his readers to prayerfully commit themselves to wrestling with the reality contained in these words: 'Search me, O God, and know my heart; test me and know my anxious thoughts. See if there is any offensive way in me, and lead me in the way everlasting' (Ps. 139:23-24).

In chapter two's exploration of 1 Samuel 16:1-13, we first read of God interacting with David in an extraordinary manner. As Samuel selects David to be Israel's new king, God impresses upon him that He is looking for someone with character, an individual whose heart is completely surrendered to Him, a person committed to integrity, transparency, loyalty, and faithfulness. 'Man looks at the outward appearance, but the LORD looks at the heart' (1 Sam. 16:7).

Since then a great deal has occurred in the life of David. As we begin to explore 2 Samuel 11, David is approximately fifty years old. The prophet Samuel, who has had a profound effect on David, has died. Saul the king and Jonathan his son, who was closer to David than a brother, have also died. David has become king over both nations of Judah and Israel.

In these intervening years, David displays courage on the battlefield, winning a number of victories; showing remarkable leadership on a national and international level, establishing Jerusalem as the nation's capital; and displaying a willingness to wait upon God's timing as he interacts with significant challenges. During those years, David becomes one of the greatest leaders in Old Testament history. On a personal level, he has everything going for him: wealth, influence, power, and the support of the nation. He is large and in charge. A time of relative peace and prosperity follows, yet sadly, as 2 Samuel 10 records, war breaks out.

Toxic Erosion

At the beginning of our study of Psalm 139, we looked briefly at the life of Saul, David's predecessor. We noticed that when Saul began to drift from God, the spiritual and moral erosion involved was slow, subtle, and silent. In 2 Samuel 11, we again see this pattern emerging. The sins that initiate a downward spiral spiritually and morally begin gradually and unobtrusively, this time not in the life of Saul, but in the life of David.

As we begin to explore 2 Samuel 11, journey back in your imagination to this now infamous chapter. Watch and consider the seductive, tranquillizing, and enslaving power of sin, in this account:

> In the spring, at the time when kings go off to war, David sent Joab out with the king's men and the whole Israelite army. They destroyed the Ammonites and besieged Rabbah. But David remained in Jerusalem. One evening David got up from his bed and walked around on the roof of the palace. From the roof he saw a woman bathing. The woman was very beautiful, and David sent someone to find out about her. The man said, 'Isn't this Bathsheba, the daughter of Eliam and the wife of Uriah the Hittite?' Then David sent messengers to get her. She came to him, and he slept with her. (She had purified herself from her uncleanness.) Then she went back home. The woman conceived and sent word to David, saying, 'I am pregnant.' (2 Sam. 11:1-5)

The remainder of the chapter reveals one startling account after another as David, known as a man after God's own heart (Acts 13:22), attempts to cover up the enormity of his sin. This incident draws us into the darkest period of his life.

David sends a note to Joab, his commander in the field, and asks for Uriah to return to Jerusalem. He hopes that Uriah will spend a few days at home, and when he later finds out that his wife is expecting, he will think he is the father, and all will be well. Although Uriah returns at the king's command, he refuses to rest at home while his colleagues are facing hardship on the battlefield. David then asks Uriah to remain a few more days and tries to get him drunk in the hope that he will then go home. After Uriah once again refuses, David sends him back to the battlefield with a letter ordering Joab to place him in the front line and then desert him, leaving him to be killed. When Bathsheba hears of her husband's death, she mourns for him; after the time of mourning is complete, David marries her and she gives birth to a son.

Now pause for a moment and ask one of those fearless, searching questions I mentioned earlier: What on earth has happened to David? In previous studies we noticed that David drew close to God amidst isolation and obscurity in his teenage years. When he faced Goliath, his profound dependence on God alone brought him victory.

We learned earlier that when everyone and everything was taken away from David, God was faithful to him, consistently renewing and refreshing his soul, answering his prayers in a spectacular fashion, and enabling him to become a military commander popular with his troops and respected by his enemies. As King David expanded his national boundaries by 60,000 square miles, he developed a strong national defense, a robust economy, and plans for a temple in Jerusalem. In terms of public admiration, he had reached the peak of popularity and enjoyed unquestioned authority, having risen from shepherd boy to Israel's greatest king. Things could not have been going better for him.

David, however, had yet to understand that the difficult times are not always when we face our greatest challenge. Difficult times often drive us to our knees, creating within us a humble, prayerful dependency on God. But pride and self-sufficiency can creep into our lives when we are successful and influential, especially when we are morally and spiritually accountable to no one.

Among the lessons learned from events in David's life, perhaps the most surprising is the potent reminder that sin is so ingenious that it does not fill us with hatred for God, but rather with forgetfulness about God. The sin that enticed David and promised him so much pleasure captured both his mind and imagination, enslaved his desires and passions, and held in captivity his ability to discern between right and wrong, leaving him addicted and shackled, a prisoner of sin.

David had allowed himself to be seduced into believing that if only he could satisfy his appetite and desires, all would be well. He had convinced himself that this was his greatest need at that moment. Like other addictions—alcohol, pornography, adultery, substance abuse, jealousy, bitterness, gossip, anger— the only way to deal with it is to stop it. Bring it to an end. Feeding the daily demands of an addictive appetite will not conquer it. David had many wives and concubines, yet he was not satisfied. Sin is always deceptive, enslaving, toxic, and addictive.

Back in chapter five when we examined Genesis 39, we saw Joseph confronted with the same temptation as David, yet he resisted, refusing to give in to the powerful appeal of what lay before him. Joseph knew he could not overcome the enticing power of sin in his own strength, and so he fled, leaving the temptation behind.

In the New Testament, the apostle Paul writes in Colossians 3:5: 'Put to death, therefore, whatever belongs to your earthly nature: sexual immorality, impurity, lust, evil desires and greed.' Notice that Paul's language instructing his readers to be utterly ruthless when it comes to sin, 'Put to death.' We should resist temptation and sin with all the strength we have, absolutely refuting its charms and seduction. There is no negotiating with sin, no rationalizing with it. No debating will conquer it. When you prayerfully run from it, dependent upon and surrendered to the power of the Holy Spirit, then—and only then—will it be conquered.

When sin first entices and attracts you, the devil never warns you of the consequences of your action; he only entices you with thoughts of excitement and pleasure, the stimulating, alluring adventure of stolen desires. He never tells the heavy drinker, 'Tomorrow morning there'll be a hangover, and ultimately you'll be ruined and lose your family.' He never tells the drug user, 'This is the beginning of a long, sorrowful, dead-end road that will ultimately dehumanize you and degrade you.'

When David was tempted, there was no mention that the result of his action would be deception, manipulation, pernicious cruelty, and murder. David's character was so badly damaged that he would tearfully regret his actions for the rest of his days. His peace vanished, his leadership was undermined, and he treated the commandments of God with indifference and contempt.

David—who had previously learned the importance of cultivating a godly character in the lonely places of obscurity and monotony; who had proven himself capable and trustworthy in the menial, insignificant, unexciting tasks of daily life; who had remained faithful to God in the face of the overwhelming challenge from Goliath, demonstrating national leadership and profound dependence on God alone—was now in danger of throwing it all away.

One of the surprising lessons to be learned from David's interaction with the manipulative and deceptive nature of sin is that, years earlier, King Saul had plotted and planned to kill David, and now David was behaving in the same manner. It could well be said that David had become Saul.

God, however, was not finished with David.

'You are the Man'

As we continue to investigate and consider the malicious nature of the events in 2 Samuel 11, the developing drama not only creates a mounting tension, but also reveals a subtle thread of concern emerging within the narrative as the passage unfolds.

Within the storyline, an inconspicuous focus on the word 'send' informs us that David appears to be in charge as he sends others to do his bidding and in the sending often determines the direction of the action and, in the case of Uriah, he is sent to his death.

Yet in the opening words of the next chapter the unfolding drama moves in an entirely new direction. It is no longer David and Joab doing the sending and receiving. Now God is taking the initiative, taking action, doing the sending. 'The LORD sent Nathan to David' (2 Sam. 12:1).

Throughout David's life, God has been faithful in the most difficult of circumstances. Previously he expressed gratitude when God refused to give up on him or to allow him to surrender to the emotion of the moment or to his circumstances. But now God is proving faithful once again when He sends Nathan to challenge David, and hold him to account for his actions.

Nathan confronts David with a memorable and vivid parable in which a rich man takes a much-loved ewe from a poor man and kills it in order to feed a guest. 'David burned with anger against the man and said to Nathan, "As surely as the LORD lives, the man who did this deserves to die! He must pay for that lamb four times over, because he did such a thing and had no pity"' (2 Sam. 12:5-6). Nathan then informs David, 'You are the man!' Nathan reveals to David the pernicious nature of his actions, highlights the contempt he has shown toward

God, and details the consequences of David's actions (2 Sam. 12:7-12).

I envisage a deeply moving moment when David comes to the point of fully realizing what he has done, with an understanding so deep, so real, and so immediate, that he grasps the magnitude of his sin. I imagine him shaking his head in horror and regret. I suspect there may have been a period of silence when time stood still as David felt incredulous about what he had done.

Through the depths of David's inner turmoil comes a moment of realization and recognition when he finally admits, 'I have sinned against the LORD' (2 Sam. 12:13). David does not try to obfuscate his responsibility, blame the circumstances, or accuse anyone else. He does not minimize his actions by saying, 'I have made a series of poor choices,' or 'I have made a mistake.' He clearly understands the significance and magnitude of what he has done. 'I have sinned against the LORD.' David is expressing not simply remorse or regret, but deep, persistent sorrow that leads to repentance and a change of heart.

At this point the emphasis within the narrative changes once again. We are powerfully reminded that the faithfulness of God also involves His refusal to abandon us to the sin that dominates our lives. His love for us is too great, too deep, too personal. His longing desire is that we would immerse ourselves in Him and enjoy the rich blessing that comes from walking with Him each day.

When David writes, 'Search me, O God, and know my heart; test me and know my anxious thoughts. See if there is any offensive way in me' (Ps. 139:23-24), he is writing from personal experience. Is he writing from a place of self-evaluation, remembering his past and grateful for God's faithfulness? He is certainly cultivating a willingness to give God access to all areas of his life, expressing a deep desire to live in a transparent manner, and seeking the refining hand of God to shape and fashion him into the man God was calling him to be.

Search Me, O God, and Know My Heart

Some time ago I received the following email. 'A friend of mine has two tickets for box seats at the Super Bowl. She paid $1,700 for each ticket. She didn't realize when she bought them that this was the same day as her wedding, and now she can't go. If you would like to go in her place, it's at Saint Peter's Church in New York City at 5:00 p.m. His name is Tom, he's six feet tall, 185 pounds, a good cook, and makes $90,000 a year. He'll be the one in the tuxedo.' What I like about this email is that I could not see the end coming.

When David surrendered to the deceitful and addictive power of his own desires, he struggled with purity, integrity, and authenticity, abused his authority, surrendered to destructive passions, demeaned and exploited Bathsheba, manipulated Joab, shamelessly conspired to kill Uriah, and sought to control everything and everyone around him. In essence David was seeking to become God, deciding who would live and who would die. But when he began this journey, he could not see how it would end.

The subtle, infectious, deception of sin is such that it does not feel like sin when we are initially attracted to it; it feels fulfilling and satisfying. David did not see that he was engaging in sin when he sent for Bathsheba or for Uriah; he felt like a king in charge of his subjects.

Somewhere along the line, he had withdrawn from a life of prayer and humility, worship and adoration, and intimacy with God. The godly activities that had once been important in his life were now a thing of the past. Actively engaging with God in a solitary place had receded into the background as obsession with self and sin had taken up residency in David's heart. The toxic deception, enticing addiction, and enslaving nature of sin had captured David and would not let him go.

But God had not given up on David and utterly refused to forsake him. God knew his heart and knew He could bring restoration and renewal into a life that had once surrendered and submitted to the rule and reign of God.

The road ahead would be painful for David. It would be distressing and distasteful. God would bring to him in a powerful and poignant manner a deep sense of personal conviction and humility, followed by relief and release. David, moved by the refining hand of God, pours out his thoughts in Psalm 51 with powerful words that leave us uncomfortable and unsettled, words that are difficult to read without being moved. 'Have mercy on me, O God, according to your unfailing love; according to your great compassion, blot out my transgressions. Wash away all my iniquity and cleanse me from my sin' (Ps. 51:1-2).

In these opening words of Psalm 51, David clearly recognizes and realizes the extent of his own sin. He at last comprehends what we so often miss: there is a world of a difference between remorse and repentance.

David understands that *he* has sinned, not someone else. His sin was no one else's fault, not caused by the circumstances of his life or the situation he found himself in. When David is exposed to the convicting power of God in the words of Nathan, 'You are the man,' he becomes aware of the damage, devastation, and horror he has caused, and he admits it. He does not seek to justify it. He does not seek to rationalize it. The Spirit of God convicts him in the deeply hidden places of his being, the secret places of his soul. It is as if the whole earth moves beneath David, and with deep repentance he cries out to a holy, loving, gracious God, 'Have mercy on me, O

God, according to your unfailing love; according to your great compassion, blot out my transgressions. Wash away all my iniquity and cleanse me from my sin' (Ps. 51:1-2).

David had slowly traded daily intimacy with God for cold indifference and apathy toward God. His wants and desires—his unbridled lust and murderous actions—had taken him to the lowest point in his life. But then came God's convicting power: 'You are the man' or 'You are the woman.' The message of the gospel is for real people who live real lives. It is never about somebody else; it's always about you, always deeply personal.

When Nathan begins the parable about the rich man stealing and killing the poor man's ewe, David assumes Nathan is talking about someone else. He feels safe in the knowledge that no one knew the extent of his sin, that nobody was watching, and he had gotten away with it. He had forgotten the lesson of long ago, 'Man looks at the outward appearance, but the LORD looks at the heart' (1 Sam. 16:7).

David becomes so aware of his sin that he can only respond by facing up to what he has done. 'For I know my transgressions, and my sin is always before me. Against you, you only, have I sinned and done what is evil in your sight, so that you are proved right when you speak and justified when you judge' (Ps. 51:3-4). David admits his sin and confesses, 'I have sinned against the LORD.' Despite the magnitude of his confession, his statement is also full of hope, full of the love and grace and goodness of God.

As David's prayer continues, he not only pours out his heart in deep and honest repentance; he also seeks restoration. 'Create in me a pure heart, O God, and renew a steadfast spirit within me. Do not cast me from your presence or take your Holy Spirit from me. Restore to me the joy of your salvation and grant me a willing spirit, to sustain me' (Ps. 51:10-12). If

David's primary desire is for cleansing, his second desire is for restoration.

When God begins to shape and refine a life, He often begins by convicting the individual of personal sin. Such an experience can be painful, yet it is always healthy. Grief over sin is followed by delight over the relief repentance brings. A humble and contrite heart is overwhelmed with the realization of the grace of God. The toxic effect of sin cannot, must not, be minimized, yet sin is incapable of taking you to a place so heinous and dark that the love of God cannot reach you.

When David prays, 'Create in me a pure heart, O God, and renew a steadfast spirit within me. Do not cast me from your presence or take your Holy Spirit from me. Restore to me the joy of your salvation and grant me a willing spirit, to sustain me' (Ps. 51:10-12), he longs for a pure heart, a heart that experiences God in all of His transforming love. David, again understanding that he cannot live a godly life in his own power, cries out for the enabling, sustaining power of God's grace. It is the same experience he writes about in Psalm 139: 'Search me, O God, and know my heart; test me and know my anxious thoughts. See if there is any offensive way in me, and lead me in the way everlasting' (Ps. 139:23-24).

Postscript

When we began exploring Psalm 139:1-2, I suggested that such a journey would not be for the fainthearted and that God may well surprise you along the way. I prayerfully trust this has been your experience and your faith has grown as you have sought to learn from this remarkable psalm.

As we come to the closing words of this psalm, 'See if there is any offensive way in me, and lead me in the way everlasting,' David encourages his readers to turn their attention to the condition of their own hearts and to ask God to lead them in the days to come.

Asking personal and probing questions is not easy, yet that is exactly what the apostle John does when he concludes his Gospel by focusing on the last recorded incident between Jesus and Peter. The event is deeply personal and comes as something of a surprise.

John chapter 20 ends with 'Jesus did many other miraculous signs in the presence of his disciples, which are not recorded in this book. But these are written that you may believe that Jesus is the Christ, the Son of God, and that by believing you may have life in his name' (John 20:30-31). These words could well be considered the perfect conclusion to John's Gospel. They contain some of the apostle's favorite words and themes— 'miraculous signs,' 'believe,' 'Jesus,' 'Christ,' 'Son of God,' 'life in his name'—as well as an invitation to believe.

Why then does John add chapter 21? What special event did John need to include in his closing chapter? In all probability writing later than Matthew, Mark, and Luke, John had the added advantage of time, and completes his Gospel in the most personal way possible.

John draws his readers into his final chapter by focusing on Jesus' reinstating Simon Peter after his threefold denial (John 18:15-18; 25-27). The chapter's opening verse transports the reader to the Sea of Tiberias, also known as the Sea of Galilee, where Simon Peter informs the disciples that he is going out to fish. John records:

> That night they caught nothing. Early in the morning, Jesus stood on the shore, but the disciples did not realize that it was Jesus. He called out to them, 'Friends, haven't you any fish?' 'No,' they answered. He said, 'Throw your net on the right side of the boat and you will find some.' When they did, they were unable to haul the net in because of the large number of

fish. Then the disciple whom Jesus loved said to Peter, 'It is the Lord!' As soon as Simon Peter heard him say, 'It is the Lord,' he wrapped his outer garment around him (for he had taken it off) and jumped into the water. The other disciples followed in the boat, towing the net full of fish, for they were not far from shore, about a hundred yards. When they landed, they saw a fire of burning coals there with fish on it, and some bread. (John 21:3-9)

John then reveals a fascinating, deeply personal account of Jesus engaging Peter in a gentle yet probing inquiry. Jesus' questions are similar to David's expressed desires: 'Search me, O God, and know my heart; test me and know my anxious thoughts. See if there is any offensive way in me, and lead me in the way everlasting' (Ps. 139:23-24).

After Peter and the disciples join Jesus for breakfast on the lakeshore, He asks, 'Simon son of John, do you truly love me more than these?' (John 21:15). It is odd that we are not entirely certain what Jesus is referring to. Was He asking Peter if he loved Him more than the other disciples? Perhaps He was asking if Peter loved Him more than his previous profession as a fisherman, pointing to the scraps of fish left over after their breakfast. When Peter responds, 'Yes, Lord, you know that I love you' (John 21:15), he is implying that his love and affection for Jesus had been clearly established. Yet Jesus asks Peter a second time, 'Simon son of John, do you truly love me?' (John 21:16). Peter again answers in the affirmative, 'Yes, Lord, you know that I love you' (John 21:16). The third occurrence gives the reader a little more insight into how Peter is feeling when John adds, 'Peter was hurt because Jesus asked him the third time' (John 21:17).

As you further explore the interaction between Peter and Jesus, the obvious question is this: Why does Jesus ask Peter the same question three times? If—as Peter believed—Jesus knew all things, why does He ask him three times? Was it that Jesus was repeating the question in order to highlight the importance and significance of the question especially in light of Peter's denial? Could it be that Peter's threefold denial of Christ earlier in the Gospel needed a threefold confession? Was Jesus gently probing into the deepest recess of Peter's soul? Was He encouraging Peter to begin to ask those fearless, searching, courageous questions, which are so similar to David's thoughts, 'Search me, O God, and know my heart; test me and know my anxious thoughts. See, if there is any offensive way in me, and lead me in the way everlasting' (Ps. 139:23-24)?

It is also worth noticing that on each occasion when Jesus asks Peter, 'Simon son of John, do you truly love me more than these?' (John 21:15), He does not address him as Peter but as 'Simon son of John' (John 21:16-17). Did Jesus address him in this way because he had forgotten that He had changed his name to Peter, or was there another reason (John 1:42)? Could it be that Jesus addressed him as 'Simon son of John' to remind him of the man he used to be, and what had occurred since they first met? Was He reminding Peter of the miracles he had witnessed, the teaching which had transformed lives, the late-night conversations around campfires at the side of the lake, Peter's own words, 'You are the Christ, the Son of the living God' (Matt. 16:16)? Yet in asking His question three times Jesus focuses on the core of the question, 'Do you love me?'

I suspect John did not want to conclude his Gospel without including the question each of us must answer. It is, of course, deeply personal and not easily answered. But if you are ever to grow in your faith and commit yourself to submitting and surrendering your life to the daily rule and reign of God, you need to answer the question Jesus asks of every person: 'Do you love me?'

Chaos and Fear

As I begin to draw this chapter to a close it is worth asking one final time, how do the closing words of Psalm 139 apply to my circumstances and the world I live in today: 'Search me, O God, and know my heart; test me and know my anxious thoughts. See if there is any offensive way in me, and lead me in the way everlasting'? (Ps. 139:23-24)

In early 2020, individuals and families responded in remarkable ways to the ripple effects of a deadly and crippling global pandemic. During this period fear and uncertainty were at times palpable.

Later that summer, as restrictions were being lifted, restaurants, shops, and stores were beginning to open. Major employers returned to work, and cautious, careful steps were taken in order to return to a measure of normality. Amidst the fears and uncertainties, it seemed there were signs of hope.

Towards the end of May 2020, however, the old infected wounds of racial injustice were reopened and became inflamed once again. The brutal and senseless deaths of members of the African-American community sparked protests across multiple cities in the USA and in other countries around the world.

Amidst deep and heartfelt cries for justice, a number of legitimate and peaceful protests were hijacked by those who wished to engage in violence, rioting, and looting. Sadly, further loss of life ensued.

Voices and Choices

How then do we seek to live out our faith in the aftermath of a global pandemic, significant unemployment, a struggling economy, and the accompanying sense of chaos and fear where life has been treated with indifference, contempt, and disdain? How do we actively and fearlessly examine our own lives and ask what action we should take amidst fears for our future and concerns over racial injustice: 'See if there is any offensive way in me, and lead me in the way everlasting'? (Ps. 139:23-24)

In the Gospel of Luke (10:25-37), Jesus tells the well-known parable of the Good Samaritan. A man traveling on the bleak, desolate desert road from Jerusalem to Jericho was attacked, robbed, badly beaten, and left 'half dead.' Jesus tells his listeners that a priest saw the man and passed by on the other side. A Levite did the same.

Then a Samaritan stopped and helped the man by treating his wounds, lifting him onto his own donkey, and taking him to an inn, where he paid for the injured man's care and lodging and promised to pay more if required. Samaritans and Jews were considered enemies; historically they despised each other. Jesus completes the parable by highlighting the personal care and concern shown by the Samaritan and challenged his listeners to 'Go and do likewise.'

We have discovered in previous chapters that Scripture teaches that throughout history we have consistently underestimated the power, significance, and magnitude of our own sin, and recently sin has been actively at work in streets of some of our major cities. It has maliciously encouraged loathing and hostility, injustice and racial attacks, looting and arson, fear and the destruction of life.

Yet the Scriptures also teach that we consistently underestimate the power, significance, and magnitude of the love of God. Such love transforms lives, refreshes and renews the soul, and births trust and intimacy, peace and contentment in a relationship with Christ. It powerfully demonstrates to individuals and societies that life is sacred and should never be treated with contempt or disdain. 'Go and do likewise.'

As a society and a culture, we now have a voice and a choice. It is easy to give voice to suspicion, blame someone else, and point accusingly in their direction. Yet suspicion and distrust are not the values we hold to be self-evident or define who we are.

We can choose to submit and surrender to fear and violence, injustice and hate, or we can stand for the core values that define who we are. Those core values have also been on display. Amidst the infectious nature of Covid-19, doctors, nurses, medical staff, police officers, and members of the emergency services, along with numerous others, selflessly served at significant personal cost. Amidst the chaos, hatred and violence of many of the protests, protesters and police walked together, knelt together, prayed together, and sung old hymns together. Both protesters and police officers intentionally intervened amidst the violence and the chaos, seeking to assist those who were injured and frightened for their lives. Those are the values that define who we are—values embedded within our humanity, 'Go and do likewise.'

As a society, choices now lie before us. Lives will be rebuilt, wounds will heal, souls will be renewed, and individuals and families will learn to love again because at the core of who we are lie the love and grace of God. His call upon us is to act as He has acted towards us. Since we have been the recipients of His transforming love and grace, there is no place for racial injustice in the Christian life. We are now called to 'Go and do likewise.'

'Go and do likewise' to all people—people of a different race, people from a different background, people who may not think as you do, or look like you. Could it be that when His love and grace are demonstrated in authentic transformed lives then the words of that ancient hymn will become a living reality for each of us. 'Amazing Grace, how sweet the sound that saved a wretch like me. I once was lost but now I'm found, was blind but now I see.'

And Finally

Throughout this book I have sought to take the principles contained in Psalm 139 and illustrate them through the lives of a number of diverse biblical characters. I trust you have enjoyed exploring each chapter and that you have been challenged about your relationship with Christ and surprised at how much you have grown as a result of time spent in the Scriptures. My prayer for you is that you will return to Psalm 139 regularly and experience the extravagant love of God on a daily basis as you come to experience afresh the realty contained in David's words, 'Search me, O God, and know my anxious thoughts. See if there is any offensive way in me, and lead me in the way everlasting' (Ps. 139:23-24).

Questions

1) In 2 Samuel 11, it is clear by David's actions that he had wandered away from daily intimacy with God. Explain why.

2) Given the serious nature of David's attempted cover-up of his affair with Bathsheba, explain why David did not confess his action and ask both Joab and Bathsheba for forgiveness.

3) Explain why is sin so powerful.

4) When Jesus asks, 'Simon son of John, do you truly love me… ?' (John 21:15), why was it important for Peter to express his love for Jesus?

5) Describe the steps you would take to develop a healthy and intimate love for Christ.